PAWSITIVE CLICKS

Teach, Play, and Bond by Clicker Training Your Cat: a Positive Reinforcement Approach

Maya Sutherland

LP Media Inc. Publishing
Text copyright © 2025
All rights reserved.

No part of this book may be reproduced or transmitted in any form or by any means, electronic or mechanical, including photocopying, recording, or by an information storage and retrieval system — except by a reviewer who may quote brief passages in a review to be printed in a magazine or newspaper — without permission in writing from the publisher.

For information address
LP Media Inc. Publishing
30012 Variolite St. NW
Princeton, MN 55371
www.lpmedia.org

Publication Data
Maya Sutherland
Pawsitive Clicks
Summary: "Teach, Play, and Bond by Clicker Training Your Cat:
a Positive Reinforcement Approach"
Provided by publisher.
ISBN: 978-1-961846-15-9
[1. Pawsitive Clicks — Non-Fiction] I. Title.

TABLE OF CONTENTS

CHAPTER 1: **Introduction to Clicker Training for Cats** 6

The basics of cat behavior and communication 8
Overview of clicker training and its benefits for cats 15
How clicker training works and the principles behind it 19

CHAPTER 2: **Getting Started with Clicker Training:**
Basic Tools and Concepts 24

Identifying and reinforcing positive behaviors 26
Shaping behavior through successive approximations 32
Tips for choosing and using a clicker 36
Tips for introducing the clicker to your cat and building
a positive, reinforcing relationship 38

CHAPTER 3: **Basic Training Techniques** 46

Teaching basic commands 47
    Here, Kitty-Kitty 50
    Sit, stay 51
Using food rewards and other reinforcers effectively 53
Building duration and distance with behaviors 55
Tips for successful training sessions and maintaining progress .. 58

Foundational Commands 60
    Target touch.. 61
    Name recognition 63
    Come recall 64
    Sit 66
    Stay 68
    Lie down 70
Skill Learning 72
    Wearing a harness 73
    Walking on a leash 74
    Mat station 76
    Brushing 78
    Nail trimming 80
    Teeth brushing 82
    Ear cleaning 84

CHAPTER 4: Advanced Commands 86

    Spin 89
    Jump 90
    Advanced jump (into your arms) 91
    High five 93
    Roll over 95
    Waving 96
    Perch 97
    Kisses 98
    Speak 99

CHAPTER 5: Clicker Training for Problem Behavior Correction 100

    Calming anxiety 103
    Scratching 104
    Counter surfing 106
    Biting/chewing 108
    Constant meowing 110
    Jumping up 112

CHAPTER 6: Clicker Training for Fun and Enrichment **114**

Dot chasing (laser pointer) 117
Guess the hand 119
Prey chasing (catching a fake mouse) 121
Bell ringing 122
Fetch 123
Tunnel run 125
Hurdle jump 126
Chair leaps 127
Figure 8 leg weave 129

CHAPTER 7: Wrapping Up **130**

Benefits of clicker training: a recap 131
Encouragement to continue training and building
a positive relationship with your cat 133

Resources for further learning and support 137

CHAPTER 1

INTRODUCTION TO CLICKER TRAINING FOR CATS

Our homes would be such peaceful, orderly places if cats would just be good boys and girls and do as they're told—but what a boring world it would be! The internet would be a far less entertaining place, for one. Just imagine: no more cats pouncing onto unsuspecting humans from great heights, no more gifts of headless rodents left in the slippers of innocent cat owners, no more cats lounging in kitchen sinks or swatting priceless objets d'art off display shelves.

However, the fact that this book has found its way into your hands likely means that you and your cat are having a hard time understanding each other. And the situation might not be all that hilarious to you anymore. On the other hand, you might simply be looking to enrich your cat's life by teaching her some tricks for fun mental stimulation or to keep her more active as she ages. Whatever your needs with training, and clicker training in particular, getting to grips with the basics of cat behavior and communication is the best place to start.

In this chapter we will look at feline body language and vocalizations and what they mean. We'll also explore what clicker training is and what makes it different from other types of training, as well as what you can teach your cat with this method. Finally, we'll go through the basics of clicker training, including the role of positive reinforcement and food rewards, as well as trust-building tips and mistakes to avoid.

The basics of cat behavior and communication

Understanding feline body language and vocalizations

Cat body language is easy to read, and the main cues are found in the ears, tail, and posture. Once you understand what each kind of body language signals, you will become more skilled at understanding or anticipating your cat's needs, as well as knowing what makes him tick.

As with human facial expressions, cat expressions lie on a spectrum, and certain expressions blend from one to the next, depending on the intensity of feeling. Think, for example, how a person's face might change from irritated or agitated to tense to worried to afraid. Once you know to look for it, you will see the same kind of nuance in feline expression.

Understanding ear posture

Let's begin with the cat's ears. When you see the ears looking pretty much neutral, upright, and facing forward but not pricked, accompanied by relaxed-looking facial features, this is, hardly surprisingly, the sign of a relaxed cat. If the ears are pricked, with the eyes widened and the pupils of the eyes potentially somewhat dilated, the cat is attentive, alert, and interested. Remember this look: an interested cat is a trainable cat. If the ears are erect and twisted to the side, the cat is tense and alert, listening for potential danger.

If those ears become twisted all the way back (looking, quite frankly, like a pair of little old horns!) your cat is annoyed or aggressive. Once the ears twist like that, you can expect to see paw swipes and nails coming out, with or without spitting, hissing, and biting. If you see ears flattened back against the skull, this is a clear sign of fear. When a cat is afraid, you will also see hissing and spitting.

Afraid

Alert

Annoyed

Relaxed

Tense and alert

Understanding tail posture

Like the ears, the cat's tail is a major communication device. An upright tail (terms and conditions apply; see "bottlebrush tail" below) is the sign of a happy cat, and you will often see this when your cat comes toward you in greeting. A quivering tail, often accompanied by chirruping sounds, is a sign of loving trust and/or playfulness, while a flicking or thumping tail is a sign of irritation.

Upright tail

Bottlebrush tail

The bottlebrush tail, typically accompanied by an arched back, claws out, hissing, spitting, and flattened ears, shows aggression and fear. As you can see, expressions of the ears, face, and tail often come in a package of body language, so there's no chance you would ever mistake an aggressive tail for the "happy-cat" flagpole tail.

Pawsitive Clicks

Understanding body posture

A body posture to take note of is lying on the back with the stomach exposed. If your cat does this with you around, it is signaling deep trust—just don't mistake it for an invitation for tummy tickles. Move in for a belly rub, and your cat will soon remind you that it is not a dog. You might be left with some scratches on your hand and a demonstration of the flicking-tail-that-signals-annoyance as your cat darts off into the next room.

Deep trust

In general, cat body postures fall into two categories: those that invite you closer and those intended to drive you away. A cat with an upright, confident body posture and flagpole tail is inviting you closer, whereas a cat in the so-called Halloween stance (arched back and bottlebrush tail) is trying to get you/a dog/another cat to move away because it is terrified.

The "go-away" postures do one of two things: they either make the cat look as large as possible, such as the Halloween stance, to frighten off the threat, or as small as possible (such as a cat crouching into itself, ears flattened completely against the skull, and tail drawn in) so as to make the cat almost invisible, causing the threat to lose sight of it.

"Go-away" posture

Understanding vocalizations

Like body language and facial expressions, cat vocalizations are an important communication tool and a clue to your cat's mood. Sounds range from soft and sweet trills and chirrups to loud and obnoxious yowls.

As with body language, vocalizations fall into two categories: those inviting others closer and those telling others to move away. Trills and chirps are usually greetings, but some cats make these sounds when they are playful, or even during a bout of play-fighting with other cats. The familiar purr is heard when a cat is relaxed and content, but also when a cat is in pain, which makes some behaviorists believe purring is a request for comfort.

The aggressive sounds—growling, hissing, spitting, shrieking, and yowling—are clear signals to get out of the cat's space. Meowing, the most classic of all cat sounds, is usually a call for attention and may signal a wide variety of requests, depending on the context. For example, "Please let me out," "Food, please," "More interesting food, please," and so on.

Interestingly, while cats definitely use their vocalizations on other cats, they just don't tend to meow at each other. It's a pretty neat thing that cats have a special sound reserved for humans, and it certainly shows that they know they're communicating with us. Even so, as many cat owners will tell you, reduced meowing is definitely something you might want to train for—and clicker training is ideal. Later in this book, we will look at how to tackle excessive meowing.

Putting it all together

When it comes to decoding your cat's body language and vocal cues, bear in mind that, like people, cats often give mixed signals. In the same way you might respond when an old acquaintance bumps into you on the street and suggests going out for coffee (you're pleased to see them, but not sure you're actually up for hanging out with them), your cat might give you mixed signals.

Getting down to the body language, you might initially smile widely, or even hug the old acquaintance (inviting behavior—although possibly with stiff arms!), but when they suggest making a date, you find yourself crossing your arms, stepping back, or putting a hand up (distancing behavior.)

In the same way, your cat might be half lying on her side, eyes half closed, legs outstretched (inviting behavior), while at the same time lightly flicking her tail and turning her ears back. Mixed signals can be confusing to you, but they're a normal part of human and animal life, and a good reminder that cats, like people, dogs, horses, and all other animals, have boundaries that need to be respected.

Some cats need more personal space than others, and if you try to scoop your cat up in your arms for a training session only to find her wriggling out of your grasp, it's a sign to back off and try again later. Trying to force a cat to do something when it doesn't want to will never ever work. Although that shouldn't come as too much of a surprise, because, in this regard, cats are, again, just like people! Even dogs, as famous as they are for wanting to please people, will snap or growl (which, again, is communication) if you're trying to coerce them into an activity they're not up for. Don't expect your cat to be any different.

Meeting your cat's physical and emotional needs

Once you understand your cat's body language, you will have more insight into her emotional needs, and this will take the human-animal relationship to a higher level. For example, imagine you didn't know that a flicking tail signaled irritation, and each time you saw your cat flicking her tail, you picked her up for a big hug, only to be swatted in the face. Now you know what that tail means, so you know to leave the cat be and give her some space. Giving her space when she's asking for it meets her emotional needs in that moment.

To maintain a positive relationship between you and your cat, you need to stay on top of both its physical and emotional needs. The physical needs—food, fresh water, shelter, safety, room to move, and a clean toilet setup—are the most obvious and straightforward to take care of. The emotional needs are the ones that start getting met once you understand your cat's communication cues.

How early experiences shape your cat

At this point it's worth noting that a cat's kittenhood has a major and lasting impact on its behavior and communication style. The time between two and seven weeks of age is an absolutely critical period for kitten socialization; age nine through fourteen weeks is also important.

Kittens that are not handled regularly (in a gentle, loving way, of course) by humans during this early window are likely to remain wild, skittish, and afraid of people into adulthood. Similarly, kittens or young cats that are abused by people will remain fearful and mistrustful as time passes.

Loving care and gentle, positive training can make a big difference even in cats that remained unsocialized in kittenhood, but the challenge will be far greater.

Overview of clicker training and its benefits for cats

What is clicker training, and how does it work?

Clicker training is a method that uses positive reinforcement to teach behavior but makes the training goal clearer and the process more efficient through the use of a sound to mark the desired behavior.

The clicker is a little handheld device that makes a click sound when you press it. The sound of the clicker is specific, and not a sound your cat hears during the normal course of events, which makes it clear and easy to immediately associate with training.

Most pet owners have some idea of positive reinforcement training, in which you give a reward when you see the pet performing the behavior you want. The idea behind giving the rewards is that it makes the animal repeat that behavior more often.

People use positive reinforcement on each other all the time. For example, if you're potty training a child, each time they go successfully, you heap praise on them. It's pretty instinctive. If you're trying to teach kids to share and you give them a piece of candy that they share as asked, then reward them with an hour of TV time, that's the same method. If your boss gives you paid time off as a reward for achieving work targets, that's positive reinforcement too.

When people think of animal training, the classic idea that comes to mind is teaching a dog to sit. (Ahem, yes, when it comes to successfully training animals, our feline friends are not the first that spring to mind!) Each time the dog sits on command, you give it a treat, and in time, the dog learns to sit on command, and you no longer need to give the treat.

But clicker training does the same thing more quickly because it eliminates confusion in the animal over exactly which behavior is being rewarded (and therefore being trained for the animal to repeat). The timing of the "yes, you did it!" / "yes, THAT's what I want" cue is crucial in animal training. In clicker training, you click; in other words, make that short, sharp sound at the exact moment you see the behavior you want. The treat follows as soon as possible afterward, but it's marking that moment with the click sound that makes the animal understand what we're after.

Picture, again, that dog learning to sit on command. Picture that excited little dog butt, wiggling about, hitting the ground, and then, "Oh my gosh, this is SO exciting, right, right?!" shooting back up into the air again. Now imagine you (very excited yourself!) give the dog a big "yes!" or "good dog!" at the moment his butt leaves the ground.

You can quickly see how confusing it is for the poor dog (or cat, because, as you will see later, yes, you can also teach your cat to sit). Timing is everything! The clicker marks the exact moment of desired behavior so that the animal knows exactly what the behavior is you want to see repeated.

Overall, the clicker is far better than voice cues because it's a neutral sound, whereas our voices mean specific things to our animals. What's more, the click is always exactly the same sound, whereas our voices change. Also, it's easier to be precise with the clicker than with spoken feedback. This clarity and consistency of timing is very beneficial to training.

The benefits of clicker training for cats

While we looked at dogs in the previous section—simply because, traditionally, more pet dogs are trained than are pet cats, so it's a familiar image to call up—this book is all about cats! And that brings us to the naysayers who will tell you that cats can't be trained. Well, they're right. Sort of.

Cats can't really be trained-trained, because they're not interested, but they can be bargained with. And this is how we teach them without having them feel they're being taught! It's a win-win situation in which both parties feel they're making the other do what they want.

While many traditional styles of training aim to control behavior, relying on dominance or the animal's desire to please, clicker training is a transaction. This is why it works especially well for cats. This is also why it strengthens the bond you and your cat share.

While some animals (read: dogs) may allow themselves to be controlled, that's not really how cats roll. But using a method with a clear payoff for the cat does work. And again, it's a very clear communication tool.

While I'm not saying your cat doesn't understand a fair bit of English, Spanish, or Greek, really, most of what we say is just waffle to our cats and dogs. Think of those Peanuts films in which the adults speak and all Charlie Brown and his friends hear is "wah-wah-wah-wah." That's probably pretty similar to what dogs and cats hear when we talk on and on, but using the clicker cuts through the waffle to let your cat know "this exact thing you're doing right now is what I want." And then: positive reinforcement; you give the treat. And soon your cat figures out this is a great game, and that you're basically a human treat dispenser and chin scratcher, and that by doing this specific thing, he can make you dispense a treat.

A brilliant bonus of clicker training is that it strengthens the bond between you and your cat precisely because she does not feel you're trying to control her. She experiences clicker training as a game, which is fun, which makes her want to keep doing it.

The method offers your cat mental stimulation as she tries to find ways to get you to click and treat. This is especially beneficial for the modern cat, which still has the old hunting drive, but for its own safety (and that of potential prey), now usually lives an indoor life.

Examples of behavior that can be taught with clicker training

Clicker training is simple and straightforward, but it can take a while for the human to get it, as we're so used to trying to correct behavior we don't want, which makes us focus on the wrong moment.

For example, most of us don't want our cats cruising the kitchen counter. But they cruise the kitchen counter because ... why wouldn't they? Often there's food, or if it's just been cleaned, there might still be an interesting smell around (or a new smell that must be analyzed), and it's nice and high up, so it's a good surveillance point, and so on. But from the human's perspective, countersurfing is not okay, so we yell as the cat is jumping up, or we make a big fuss while the cat is up there.

For clicker training, these are not the moments to mark. On the contrary: you need to be patient and bide your time, click at the moment your cat jumps off (of its own volition), and then provide the treat as its feet strike the ground. And repeat.

The cat associates your arrival, clicker in hand (and later no clicker in hand), with the treat or pat, and so jumps off the counter on seeing you. You can teach all manner of behaviors with the clicker, from jumping through a hoop to touching a target to sitting or staying to jumping into the carrier to scratching the scratch post instead of your antique sofa.

Here are some behaviors you can teach your cat using the clicker:
- Come (the simplest command is the best place to start)
- Touch target (the starting point for all other clicker teaching)
- Go to mat
- Scratch this, not that (saving your furniture)
- Perch here, not there (staying off tables and countertops)
- Sit (do not teach this one first; your cat will think you're rewarding it for sitting still, and that puts a handbrake on further training. See Chapter 3 for order of training.)
- Sit pretty
- High five
- Wave

How clicker training works and the principles behind it

The role of positive reinforcement in clicker training

You will recall that we looked at positive reinforcement above, and it's such a core component of clicker training that it bears repeating. Rewarding wanted behavior causes that behavior to be repeated. This works for people or animals, and the reward can come in the form of praise, food, or friendly touch, such as stroking your cat's back or tickling behind her ears.

With positive reinforcement, the animal learns that when it does something specific (such as walking past the sofa to scratch its scratch post instead), that action/behavior leads to a reward. So, in a nutshell, in positive reinforcement, positive behavior earns positive consequences. This is the opposite of punishment, which is often used in outdated, fear-based training systems. (To be clear, in training, punishment means the unwanted behavior is followed by negative consequences, such as shouting or physical punishment.) In training, positive reinforcement is the most successful approach because it amounts to working with your cat or dog instead of against it. What's more, punishment only leads to fear, which breaks trust and makes the animal want to get away from you. For successful training, never shout, and at all costs, avoid the smacking or other physical harm that was viewed as acceptable in previous generations.

To recap the connection between positive reinforcement and clicker training: The clicker marks the exact behavior you want. As soon as possible after this moment—marked with the audible click—you provide the treat. The animal associates the action with the sound and the sound with the treat, and that makes for quicker, more efficient training because you've marked the moment.

How to use the clicker and rewards to shape behavior

Over time, the clicker and rewards can be used to shape behavior. In training (of all kinds, not just animal training, but in learning to play tennis, play the piano, tap dance, speak a new language, etc.), "shaping" means using reinforcement little by little to get closer to the ideal behavior or performance. Shaping is especially useful in teaching your cat to do tricks, where you build the trick up move by move over time. We will look at this in more depth in Chapter 2 (shaping) and Chapter 6 (tricks).

Shaping is a process of breaking down a complex move or behavior into simple steps, repetition and selection. You, as the trainer, select the behavior or action you want to see. For example, imagine you are teaching your cat to high five. Think of the shape of this move: the cat must lift its paw off the ground, turn the paw all the way to a vertical position, and then bat the paw forward to meet yours.

In shaping the high five, you will begin with getting your cat to simply lift its paw slightly off the ground. A lift earns a click and treat just for the basic little lift. As you continue, you no longer click for a little lift, but wait until you get a higher lift, and then click that, and so on, until you have shaped the entire move. We will look in more detail at training the high five in Chapter 6.

Shaping takes time, patience, and repetition over days and weeks. Do bear in mind that training sessions must remain short. For a cat, two minutes of training is a long session. What's more, if you're rewarding with treats, you could reward your cat into obesity if you're trying to train for an hour a day!

The main takeaway here is that clicking marks the exact moment of "yes, that's what I want to see!" thus firmly implanting the memory (and positive association with the reward) in the cat's mind. With shaping, little by little, that "yes, that's what I want" shifts to the slightly more advanced part until you've built up a full move, such as a high five or jumping through a hoop.

The importance of timing and consistency in clicker training

As mentioned before, the click marks—for the cat—the exact moment of success, so that it knows exactly what you want it to repeat. You're marking not only an action but also a momentary choice. You can think of it in visual terms, like a snapshot.

If you want to teach your cat to leave your sofa and scratch the scratch post instead, you click as the cat strides past the sofa (snapshot) and again as it reaches for the scratch post (snapshot). Imagining it in terms of a photo click can help you to mark the moment.

Being accurate with timing is critical. Imagine, again, teaching the high five. Say your cat has lifted its paw, but in the next instant puts down the paw and shakes its head. If you click now, you're teaching your cat you want it to shake its head!

It takes most people a while to get the hang of timing, so it might be worth practicing on your own, away from the cat. For example, go outside with a friend and ask them to toss a pebble into the air so you can click the exact moment the pebble hits the ground. And repeat. Luckily, using the clicker is much more accurate than praise or voice cues, even if you have to start with an initial bit of training yourself.

Introduction to Clicker Training for Cats

TIPS FOR BUILDING TRUST AND RAPPORT WITH YOUR CAT THROUGH CLICKER TRAINING

Cats are smart, and they have a long memory, which is absolutely to your advantage if you are thoughtful in your training, but disastrous if you get cranky or impatient. By rushing, you risk confusing your cat, and by shouting or punishing, in effect, you are teaching your cat you are not to be trusted. If your cat doesn't trust you, she, at best, won't play along and, at worst, will flat-out avoid you! Here are ways to teach trust and keep your cat in the learning zone:

- **Be patient.** It takes lots of repetition over numerous short training sessions to redirect behavior. Don't rush your cat.
- **Choose the right time to train.** Look at your cat's body language. Is she relaxed but alert? If not, wait.
- **Quit while you're ahead.** End your training session on a high—or neutral—note. Don't stress your cat out by trying to coax her into doing more when she's had enough.
- **Feeling frustrated? Pack it in for the day.** Don't try to train your cat when you're frustrated, agitated or mad.
- **Remember, this is not about controlling your cat.** The two of you are working together, in partnership, to form new behaviors more than changing old ones.

Common mistakes to avoid

With the introductory ideas from this chapter in your tool kit, you're almost ready to start training your cat! Before you begin, bear in mind these common mistakes.

- **Long training sessions.** Keep it short: your cat's attention span is short, and longer than a couple of minutes of training is usually too long. Intersperse training sessions throughout the day. You might get up to three to four minutes of training in total per day.
- **Focusing on "bad" instead of "good" behavior.** Ignore the undesired behavior (e.g., jumping onto the counter) and click on the desired (e.g., jumping off).
- **Boring treats.** Dry kibble is boring. Tiny little cubes of cooked chicken are delicious.
- **Training right after a good meal.** Treats are less interesting on a full belly.
- **Clicking too late.** It's easy to get the timing wrong and click when your cat is already on his next move. Don't worry, you're training yourself here too. You'll get more accurate as you go!

Introduction to Clicker Training for Cats

CHAPTER 2

GETTING STARTED WITH CLICKER TRAINING: BASIC TOOLS AND CONCEPTS

Before we start, you need to learn a bit more about the key concepts of clicker training, and of course, the tools. We'll talk about what exactly a clicker is, the different forms they may take, and how and why using an actual clicker is more successful than vocal cues or praise.

First of all, you need to get clear with yourself on what exactly it is that you want your cat to learn. Of course, many people have visions of cute tricks and nifty circus acts (high-fiving the dog; bursting spectacularly through a sheet of rice paper attached to a hula hoop). However, we must all learn to walk before we can run; clicker training is no exception.

As with anything in life — cleaning the yard, renovating your home, learning to figure skate — training needs to be broken up into little steps. You need to learn the basics first. It's plain to see how trying to train for a Lutz or triple Axel on the ice before you can even skate forwards would likely end in mayhem and hospital bills.

Thus we're going to break training down into steps. And we're going to start with the basics first. Always.

Before getting into tricks and other higher-grade matters, you're simply going to start with what already works. And reinforce it.

Cat comes when you call her? Great! You're going to reinforce that.

Cat cutely trots up the stairs behind you to join you at bedtime? Reinforce. Check!

Cat jumps on the table and tries to share your breakfast with you? You will work on that, later, and solve it too, with clicker training, only not just yet.

Identifying and reinforcing positive behaviors

How to identify and reinforce positive behaviors in your cat

Identifying positive behaviors

First off, we get clear on the behaviors we want. Most of us think of our pets as being "good" or "bad," because that's how most of us were raised by our parents. However, it's going to save you a lot of headaches, not to mention strengthen your bond with your cat, if you make a bit of a paradigm shift in that department.

Instead of thinking "good" or "bad," think "desirable" (to me, the owner) and "undesirable" (to me and the good-manners police in general). Cats, like dogs, chimpanzees, dolphins, hippos and any other animal out there, are not governed by human laws of "good" and "bad."

What does drive animals? Behaviors that benefit them. Acquiring good things (food, water, cardboard boxes, their favorite toys, petting and stroking — sometimes — being given their space — other times) and avoiding bad things (loud noises, physical force, certain smells, aggressive people or animals, in some cases new people or animals, car rides, the vet, unsatisfactory perches, etc.)

Just give yourself some slack and realize that understanding exactly what works for your cat may not be what you first expect.

Think of the last time you got your cat an expensive birthday gift. Remember how the gift got dismissed with nothing but a "well, meh," whereas the box got a tremendous "oh, myyyy!" What motivates a cat can often defy human logic.

In retraining behaviors you don't want, you're going to think laterally, or, "out of the box" (pun intended!) But I'm getting ahead of myself. We will cover that in Chapter 5 (Clicker Training for Problem Behaviors).

For now, the focus is on reinforcing the behaviors you do want to see, beginning, as mentioned above, with positive behaviors that your cat already exhibits. These behaviors may include:

- Coming when called
- Not shredding the sofa
- Sauntering peacefully past the dog without hissing or claws coming out
- Not kicking or fussing when you pick them up or handle them
- Waiting nicely as you serve their dinner (instead of tripping you and getting in your way as you're preparing it)
- Accepting cuddles

Note that your cat may or may not be doing these things already. The point is, if they're doing them, reinforce them. If they're not yet doing them, hang tight. We'll get to that later.

Reinforcing positive behaviors

In Chapter 1, we looked at the mechanics of reinforcement, and specifically positive reinforcement. To recap: when your cat does something you want, you strengthen that behavior (and ensure your cat repeats it, more and more) by giving them something they value.

Example: You want your cat to come to you, so you call it. The cat comes, and you hand it a treat. This is positive reinforcement. Remember, in clicker training, you click at the exact moment of the desired behavior, and then follow that with the treat.

In summary: Acknowledge to yourself the behaviors you already see as positive. Make a list. Pay attention to your cat. Take note of the "good" behavior you see and reinforce it with the click-and-treat method.

Positive reinforcement: a step-by-step exercise

To help you get going, here are some ideas. Think of it as helpful prep work.

What to do: Spend Day 1 of your process — before the actual training even begins — looking for as many opportunities as possible to reinforce the positive behaviors your cat already exhibits. Make yourself a chart of behaviors that you can check off as you go.

As an example, here are the positive behaviors listed above. Some of them your own cat might already be doing on the regular, so that's great! If your cat is not exhibiting any of these behaviors, just ignore those items.

Remember, at this point we're not training yet. We're only reinforcing what's already there. We have included some blank rows where you can fill in any other positive behaviors your cat displays that we have not mentioned here.

The second column is for checking off your success. Each time your cat displays the positive behavior, click and treat (be precise with your timing!). Then make a check mark in the column.

Since cats don't perform well under pressure (after all, not many of us do …) we haven't included a number of checks to shoot for. Instead, stay alert and keep the clicker and treats at hand.

It's your job to be vigilant: (a) noticing the behaviors and (b) reinforcing through click-and-treat, with super precise timing. It's your cat's job to just be himself.

That said, it's seriously motivational to see check marks stacking up, so let them. And, if you're vigilant, they will. Tip: If you constantly have your attention divided — for some of us that means focusing on Netflix or the football game, for most of us it means having our eyes glued to the phone screen — your success will be far lower.

For best results, pay attention to your cat fully. That's not to say you have to give up the entire rest of your life. But make time for just you and your cat. Five minutes here and five minutes there of dedicated focus are the building blocks to success.

Positive behavior intro assignment

Positive behaviors	Check as you go
Coming when called	☐
Not shredding the sofa	☐
Sauntering peacefully past the dog without hissing or claws coming out	☐
Not kicking or fussing when you pick them up or handle them	☐
Waiting nicely as you serve their dinner (instead of tripping you and getting in your way as you're preparing it)	☐
Accepting cuddles	☐
	☐
	☐
	☐
	☐

The importance of reinforcing positive behaviors in your cat

By strengthening those positive behaviors you cat is already exhibiting, you'll notice a number of benefits. First of all, it makes life easy for both you and your cat: you are focusing on the positive instead of the negative. Nobody is getting rubbed up the wrong way. Reinforcing the positive will never end in tears.

Reinforcing these positive behaviors is a great way to ease into training. What's more, it builds trust and confidence in a win-win cycle. This then strengthens the bond you and your cat share, which will not only make future training easier, but is also one of the primary joys of having a pet in the first place.

It also introduces your cat the clicker-training method, namely: When I do this exact thing, I get a click. Click equals treat. And then the penny drops: Oh, I can make my human click-and-treat! All I have to do is this specific thing. Bingo!

A great part of reinforcing positive behaviors is that you are guaranteed no pushback. The focus on the positive is crucial in clicker training, and it will help you make that shift in mindset. As discussed above, most of us gravitate immediately to correcting "bad" behavior. But this mindset is contrary to positive reinforcement, and therefore to clicker training.

In clicker training, we first reinforce the positive behaviors, and later on work on the negative behaviors we don't want to see (Chapter 5). Even then, we are not correcting or changing behavior as much as we are guiding the animal into making (for themselves) the choices that work for us, the human. This principle of guiding and not forcing is vital to successful clicker training.

TIPS FOR REINFORCING BEHAVIORS CONSISTENTLY AND EFFECTIVELY

As pointed out in Chapter 1, you're going to take things slowly. Keep training times short. Two minutes, two or three times a day is plenty. It might be tempting to try longer sessions given reinforcing positive behavior is a relatively simple task, but trying to keep your cat engaged for longer than just a minute or two at a time won't work.

When it comes to effective training, consistency is key. Inconsistency sends mixed messages. Here are some tips:

- Begin by choosing ONE behavior to reinforce, e.g., coming when called.
- Be precise with the timing of the clicker: click at the moment your cat starts moving in your direction.
- Always click at the "yes" moment; treat follows.
- After a successful "come on being called" take a few steps away and repeat.
- If your cat ignores you, stop. Don't try to force them into doing anything.
- Be patient, with your cat and with yourself.
- Spend several days on just this one behavior.
- Wait for this behavior to be solidly reinforced before starting to reinforce the next.

Shaping Behavior through Successive Approximations

What is shaping, and how does it work in clicker training?

Shaping is the step-by-step process in which we reach our training goals. It comes down to taking a positive tendency and reinforcing it through repetition to work towards the ultimate goal little by little.

Shaping is not unique to animal training. Coaches and instructors of all kinds use shaping to teach and improve performance. If you're learning to shoot a basketball, your coach will instruct you in the correct method first: stand with your feet no further than shoulder width apart, slightly staggered, knees flexed, etc. They will then use the principles of shaping to train you: first having you master the basic stance, and separately from that, how to hold the ball, then, how to propel yourself forward.

You would then learn to shoot from close by the goal, and later on from further away. Shooting depends on distance (how much strength to put behind the throw versus how much to hold back) as well as direction (aim). An effective coach would drill you on these two aspects separately.

Back to cats: if, for example, you wanted to train your cat to jump through a hoop, you would first train her to simply move towards the hoop. Once she reliably moves towards the hoop, you can start training the jump. You would start with the hoop on the ground, and then, after she successfully and consistently moves through the hoop, slowly, over a number of sessions, position the hoop slightly higher and higher until you reach the goal height.

Clicker training is an effective way of shaping behavior, because the click clearly communicates what you are reinforcing. It makes it clear to your cat exactly what you want, so that they can learn to repeat that behavior.

Examples of shaping in action

Building on the example of the hoop-jumping trick: If your cat is consistently jumping through the hoop when you hold it an inch off the ground, you can increase the challenge to an inch and a half, or two inches, without a problem. If, however, you suddenly raise the hoop a foot off the ground, you can expect the cooperation to end.

This may seem odd, because you know your cat can jump at least five feet in the air without breaking a sweat. That is a different matter, though. What the cat is doing for you during training sessions is not the same as what it does for itself, on its own schedule.

It's worth pointing out that in training you're not always working with the animal's actual ability — which is usually far beyond the work you're doing together. Instead, you're working within the range of what the animal has been doing for you, in training.

In shaping, you are communicating to the animal what you want, and in reality, you're shifting the rules little by little:

- First I want you to sprint up to me
- Second, I want you to sprint a little past me up to this hoop on the ground
- Third, I want you to jump through it too
- Fourth, I'm raising it an inch off the ground and I want you to jump through that, etc.

The role of the clicker in all of this is, of course, the reinforcement. Right at the start, when all you're training for is the cat moving up to the hoop, you click and treat to reinforce.

Later on, when you have the cat stepping through the hoop, you click only at that point and no longer to reinforce the initial movement towards the hoop. That part is already reinforced.

In all of this, keep sight of the positive reinforcement. Cat jumps through the hoop: Click.

Cat saunters up to the hoop only to sniff it and do an about turn: Ignore. Don't say anything, don't try to steer the cat's body or pick it up and lift it through the hoop. This is ineffective and confusing.

Remember, the goal is always to reinforce the positive behavior. Ignore the rest.

TIPS FOR SHAPING BEHAVIORS SUCCESSFULLY AND MAINTAINING PROGRESS

There are a few rules to bear in mind when it comes to good shaping. These include:

- Take it slow: raise the bar little by little so your cat can always realistically achieve what you're asking him to.
- Focus on one criterion at a time — don't try to shape two at once. (In the hoop training example, movement through the hoop and height of the jump in separate sessions.)
- Use intermittent reinforcement: Once your cat has reliably learned the criterion you're training, click-and-treat only some of the time, not every single time. This is how you keep up the behavior/performance at the current level. Once you're not click-treating for each success, that frees you up to reinforce only the best examples of the move/of the behavior. [For a fun story about intermittent reinforcement, read on.]
- When starting to train a new aspect, temporarily relax the standards on the previous ones. For example, in hoop training, imagine you've reached the point of adding a sheet of rice paper to the hoop for you cat to jump through. This is a major new challenge. The previous challenge was hoop height. So now, begin by lowering the hoop if not right down to the ground, just a quarter of an inch from the floor.
- End training sessions on a high note — after a moment of progress, which often means ending the session a little sooner than you think you should. Never, ever end with scolding or stomping off in a huff.

Tips for choosing and using a clicker

Finding the right clicker

The clicker is a very simple device: basically, a small plastic box with a button that makes a two-toned clicking sound when you press it. There are plenty of different brands and designs, but all do the same thing, and really it comes down to personal preference.

Some clickers make a louder sound than others. If your cat is easily startled, a softer clicker might be better; for a cat that is hard of hearing, a louder clicker would be better. Some clickers have rounded corners to make them lie more comfortably in your hand, while others come with a fabric loop that fits around your finger or wrist.

Any clicker that produces a short, crisp click is fine for the job. Clickers are widely available online and in stores. As with anything in life, it's worth going to the store yourself to see what you prefer in real life. But there isn't a "correct" clicker, the perfect clicker is the one that works the best for you and your cat.

How to properly use the clicker to signal a reward

Timing is everything. The most important job (and only job) for the clicker is to mark the moment of success. It's a communication tool that tells your cat "this exact thing is what I want."

For example, if you want your cat to come to you, the movement towards you is what you want to reinforce. If you call and click immediately, before your cat has started moving, the cat will think you're rewarding it for sitting still. Ditto if you click too late, once your cat has stopped moving.

So, again, the clicker marks the moment, and the treat is the reward. But because they come as a pair, the cat associates the click with the treat. Always, always click first, then give the treat.

To engage your cat, ensure you're offering tasty treats, such as tiny cubes of cooked chicken, rather than dry or stale kibble. If you really want to show your cat you're pleased with something he has done, give more treats, not more clicks. The click is always just a single click.

Once your cat learns that certain behaviors earn clicks (and therefore treats) he or she will start displaying that behavior more and more, spontaneously. If you love it when your cat rolls over with a cute chirrup, click as she does that, then treat. You'll probably begin to notice that she starts doing it more often of her own accord.

Tips for introducing the clicker to your cat and building a positive, reinforcing relationship

How to introduce the clicker to your cat in a way that builds trust and confidence

Forcing your cat to do things will harm trust and confidence. So will trying to get them to do things that are too advanced before they are ready (an example, again, from the human world — trying to learn the Axel before you've mastered basic skating).

Remember the first point of shaping. The goal in each session needs to be easy enough for your cat to realistically achieve success. Luckily it's easy to avoid forcing and overreaching if you're simply aware of it.

Step-by-step Clicker Training Session (an example)

So, now that you've reminded yourself what not to do, it's time to get going with the rest.

Start with a hungry cat. If your cat has just had a meal (or if you're free feeding, leaving kibble out all day), he won't have space for more than one or two treats in his stomach. In that case, you won't get very far. If you free feed, put the food away two to three hours before you want to begin training.

2 **Get your treats ready.** Little cubes of cooked chicken or fish, or even small cubes of cheese, work well. Have them where you can reach them easily. Now gather up your clicker and cat, and begin.

3 **The first thing you will do is called "charging" the clicker.** By this we mean teaching the cat that the sound of the click equals "treat." Get your cat's attention (if he's hungry and notices you have a treat in your hand, you'll have his attention.) Now click and provide the treat at exactly the same moment. You could hold the treat in your open hand, or toss it a foot or so away so that the cat has to move to get to it; click at the same moment as tossing the treat.

4 **Repeat the simultaneous click and treat three or four times.** Then you can start to build in a gap of a second between the click and the treat, but always click first. Click, then treat. This is all you're doing: don't talk to the cat, try to touch it or try to make it look at you, just click-treat.

5 **Stop when your cat gets bored.**

How long you work on this "clicker charging" exercise will depend on your cat. As soon as he looks bored or not interested, stop. Remember that your training sessions will always be short. It might take your cat a few sessions before the penny drops and he makes the glorious discovery that something he himself is doing is causing the click, and therefore the treat.

Once that link has been established in the cat's mind, training can start.

In Chapter 3 we will look at your first piece of training: target touching. This is hardly a trick, but it's an unbeatable entry point to clicker training, because it's easy, straightforward, and uses your cat's natural curiosity as the launchpad to training.

TIPS FOR BUILDING A REINFORCING RELATIONSHIP WITH YOUR CAT THROUGH CLICKER TRAINING

In training, you and your cat are in a partnership. To keep things going smoothly:

- Never try to force your cat to do anything. In trying to get the cat to perform a certain action or behavior, what you are really doing is trying to elicit a choice. When the cat makes the choice you intended (e.g. sitting nicely while you dish up his dinner), click and treat. When the cat makes the choice you don't want to see, don't make a fuss.
- Remember to respect your cat's need for space. Use her body language and vocal cues as clues to her needs.
- Be patient. Rushing your cat will get you nowhere, and in fact, only set you back.
- Be aware that your cat has to make certain links in his own mind. It might take repetition before he gets something, but he needs to — and will — draw the right conclusions in his own time.
- Be teammates, not adversaries. Remember the two of you are on the same side!

Common mistakes to avoid when introducing the clicker and building a reinforcing relationship

Positive reinforcement is the foundation of clicker training, so perhaps the most important rule is to never punish or scold your cat for negative behaviors. Other important tips:

- Avoid training sessions outside of when your cat is hungry.
- Don't be impatient.
- Don't expect big changes overnight.
- Don't try to cram all your training into one day of the week. Space sessions evenly throughout the week.
- Don't expect long training sessions. A few minutes at a time will suffice. Dogs, horses and other animals can be trained for longer, but cats like short sessions.

Busting myths about clicker training

"Clicker training is difficult."

✗ It's not: it just takes awareness of the principles, understanding of how positive reinforcement works, love and respect for your cat, and a bit of patience.

"Clicker training is too advanced for me — it's for experts only."

✗ Nope. You too, can train your cat using a clicker!

"The clicker is there to get my cat's attention."

✗ No, the clicker is there to pinpoint the exact behavior you are reinforcing (with a treat).

"If I train my cat using a clicker, I will always have to carry a clicker."

✗ That's not true. Once your cat has made certain connections in his mind, the clicker is no longer necessary. It's just a training tool.

"Clicker trainers use positive training — they don't believe in discipline."

✗ That's untrue. Positive doesn't mean permissive, but it does mean taking the route that avoids harsh punishment (scolding, physical force), instead guiding the animal into personally making the choices that work for you, the owner. The kinds of discipline positive trainers use include vocal interrupters (instead of shouting or scolding), time-outs, ignoring the unwanted behavior, or taking away something the animal wants (such as a favorite toy).

More tips for clicker training success

- Choose delicious treats; and cut them into tiny portions.
- Be mindful of how much your cat is eating overall in a day. A training session might replace a whole, or half of, a meal.
- Click during the behavior you want, not after.
- At the very start of your training, at the "clicker charging" stage, you click and provide the treat at same the exact moment.
- A little later on, a short space between clicking and giving the treat is fine. But you still always click first, then treat.

A Little Tale (Cautionary) of the Explosive Power of Intermittent Reward

I first became aware of the power of intermittent reward when one of my cats, "Fluffy Boy," demonstrated the unique skill that many cats have to herd their owners.

The situation: I had in the house a bag of cat treats. After the first treat, Fluffy Boy knew exactly where I stashed this kitty crack, and would frequently march up to the pantry and start demanding his share.

His voice was piercing; his Siamese ancestry coming through loud and clear. Unfortunately, my husband and I reinforced this behavior by unwittingly carrying out the intermittent reward system. (See "Tips for shaping behavior" above for more on intermittent rewards, which is something you can absolutely use to your advantage in training, unless you're a greenhorn at it. My husband and I were greenhorns back then. After reading this book, you will not be.)

By switching between "Oh no, he cannot have any more, he's already had way too much! No, Fluffy Boy, no!" and thirty minutes later, caving, "Oh my soul, how this howling is wearing me down! OK FB, just one more, there you go, oh my GOODNESS aren't you cute gobbling that down ..." — by doing this, we were only reinforcing the behavior through intermittent rewarding.

Now, that isn't even the end of the story. To clarify: the pantry is located at the base of the stairs. Soon Fluffy Boy's jonesing got so bad that when I would head upstairs for the night, he would leave his post at the pantry door, dash after and ahead of me on the stairs, and literally try to stop me from going up by placing his body between my leg and the next step. When I sidestepped him, he'd only leap up again, weaving through my legs, pausing only to meow loudly and turn his head down towards the pantry. That was when I told my husband we might have a problem. But then I'd get upstairs, go to sleep and forget about it. Still not the end of the story.

One fine day, somebody in the house left the pantry door ajar. FB, sadly for him, was occupied with a previous engagement (practicing the art of decorative sleeping), and Little Dog sauntered in, grabbed the whole bag of Kitty Crack and scarfed it all down in one big hoovering.

This episode ended in spectacular digestive upset for Little Dog, and even more spectacular emotional upset for mop-and-bleach-in-hand humans. And that was the end of the Kitty Crack. That's how we inadvertently learned about intermittent rewarding, and how to avoid the pitfall of the "cat training the humans".

CHAPTER 3
BASIC TRAINING TECHNIQUES

Now that you have the foundational theory under your belt, you're just about ready to start training! You're going to start modestly, by teaching basic commands. Once you and your cat have mastered the basics, you can work your way up to fancier things like tricks, as well as redirecting unwanted behaviors.

Teaching basic commands

The importance of teaching basic commands in clicker training

In Chapter 2, we spent a lot of time talking about why it's important to start small. When it comes to clicker training, a solid foundation is vital, and that's where basic commands come in.

Trainers typically find that the first behavior any animal learns in clicker training sticks with them the best and acts as a "fallback" behavior. That means you have to think carefully about what behavior you want to teach first before you start training. For example, if you teach the "sit" command before anything else, your cat may think you are rewarding it for sitting still. Going forward it may try to "sit still" every time it's confused, thinking this is the behavior you want it to be performing.

Similarly, if you first teach a behavior that your cat can do independently, for example rolling onto his side, this action will become their "fallback" behavior. Then, whenever your cat becomes confused about what you want from it with a click, he's likely to perform this action of rolling onto his side.

For this reason, "touch target" is the very first behavior we teach in clicker training. It works well because the target is a prop we can bring out or put away. This makes it clear to the cat that we are clicking for a specific action we are eliciting from it — not a random action on the cat's part.

Examples of basic commands that can be taught using clicker training (e.g., "sit," "stay," "come")

It all begins with the target touch

Since teaching "sit" and "stay" early on are counterproductive, the first command we teach is "come." In reality, "touch target" is the first version of "come" we teach. Before reading this book, you may have thought that teaching a targeting command was unnecessary, but it's actually a foundational command in cat training!

To teach "touch target," begin with your target, about a dozen fresh treats cut up into pea-sized bits, your clicker, and a hungry cat. Remember that you will have to have "charged" the clicker (see Chapter 2) in previous training sessions over the course of a few days. If you have neglected charging the clicker, you will be simply setting off on the road to nowhere with one thoroughly confused cat.

For your target, use a wooden spoon, pencil, stick or chopstick. Begin this session by reinforcing that click spells treat, in other words, click and give the treat at the same moment. Your cat is likely to realize you're onto a good thing here.

Repeat the "charge up" a handful of times. Remember to click and treat simultaneously the first few times, then click and, after a delay of a second or two, give the treat. Always click first, treat after.

Now get your target stick. Hold it out, about two or three inches in front of your cat's nose. Cats are naturally inquisitive, and like to make sense of things by smelling them, so it's likely your cat will touch her nose to the target. Excellent! Click at the moment of touch, move the target out of sight, then treat. Repeat several times to reinforce.

If your cat doesn't seem interested in the target after all, rub a little food on the tip, and that should be enough enticement. Also, instead of holding it out a couple of inches, bring the target close to your cat's nose, so that they almost have to touch it.

A touch or bump to the target scores a click, scores a treat.

Once the cat has successfully touched or bumped the target up close a few times, and you've clicked and rewarded accordingly, start moving the target a little further away. This way, your cat must actively step forward to get to the target.

It aids the learning process if your cat hears the click while she is moving, because she realizes that the click was indeed the result of something she did, and not a random thing.

While "touch target" isn't a classic command, it leads in to the commands. And it's a nifty way of getting your cat to move in a direction of your choosing. Once he has learned to step up to the target when you've moved it an inch or two away, you can proceed to move it a foot or two, until your cat learns to follow the target as you move it along.

In this way, you will be able to get your cat to jump off furniture (or on, like a circus kitty) as you lead it with the target, like a magic wand. You'll be able to get him to march into his carrier, or out of it.

HERE, KITTY-KITTY

Teaching your cat to come has obvious practical advantages, but it's also important for your cat's safety. Say your cat slips out of the apartment and gets lost in the building, or darts into the neighbor's yard, a successful recall cue can save you and your cat hours of "my-cat-has-gone-missing!" distress. (Recall is the word trainers use for getting an animal to come to you when called.)

If you already have a dog who readily comes to you when you use the word "come," you may want to use a cat-specific sound instead. This will avoid a stampede of dog(s) and cat(s) rushing at you all at once. For cats, many trainers like to use a double tap of the knuckles on the nearest hard surface as their recall cue.

Be sure the sound is different from a knock on the door, because that would confuse the cat, and cause it to dart to the door whenever someone comes. That's a behavior most people try to train their dogs out of, so training the cat to do it instead would be bizarre.

While you will still be using the clicker method for the recall, in this case you begin with the rap/tap sound.

The principle remains the same: we summon the cat (rap), click when it starts moving toward us and reward it with a treat to reinforce the behavior.

1. Double tap your knuckles on a hard surface to make the "rap/tap" sound.
2. Wait for your cat to come to your hand holding the treat.
3. Reward the cat with the treat immediately once they come.

Whereas in target touching we are creating a new behavior and shaping it, with the recall we are taking an existing behavior, but ensuring a reliable, consistent response to our signal.

Always reward a successful recall immediately. Don't, however, reward if your cat initially ignores you. What you reward, persists. If you provide a treat when the cat comes only on your third or fourth call, you are training him to come only on a third or fourth call.

In other words, cat comes on first call: treat. Cat ignores you, and saunters along on the fifth call, ignore cat back. No cussing, no fussing, just an ignore for an ignore. And note, that's not to be spiteful, it's just to avoid reinforcing unwanted behavior!

SIT, STAY

The main reason for teaching sit or stay are practicality. Very often, our cats get in the way — seemingly trying their best to literally get under our feet — when we are doing things around the house. For everyone's safety, it's good to have "sit, stay" in the repertoire of trained behaviors.

Teach "sit and stay" only after touch target and recall are well established. Get your clicker, treats and hungry cat lined up. Choose a spot that (a) is safely out of the way and (b) the cat will like. You might choose a high chair, or your cat's cat tree.

Entice your cat to the spot either by leading it with your wand, erm, target, or by placing a treat where you want it to go. Click as it jumps up, and then give another treat. Silently count to three. If the cat is still seated, click and treat again.

Keep this going. Once the cat has finished its treat, if it is still sitting, count a few more seconds this time, then click and treat again. Once the behavior is established, and the cat is doing it spontaneously for clicks, you can add in the spoken cue: "Up!" or "Stay!" when you want your cat to take his place.

TIPS FOR TEACHING BASIC COMMANDS EFFECTIVELY AND CONSISTENTLY

- Keep the timing exact: click at the exact moment of the desired behavior.
- Begin by training target touching, even if it's tempting to skip because it's not flashy.
- Train one animal at a time. Close the door to keep out people and other animals, which are a distraction.
- Keep training sessions short. Your cat is not up for marathons. Short, even very short, sessions, once or twice every day, will pay dividends.
- Don't anthropomorphize your cat: If she's not doing what you're after, she's not being stubborn, lazy or conniving, she simply hasn't learned the cue fully yet.
- Remain patient, especially if your cat previously only heard the cue "Come" for things it didn't like: getting into the carrier, going to the vet, the groomer, etc.
- Don't vary your cues: If you use the word "Come" to call your cat, keep to that. Don't confuse her by sometimes saying "Here" or "Come here." If you're using the rap/knock, always do that — don't sometimes change to a word.

Using food rewards and other reinforcers effectively

Since clicker training is based on positive reinforcement, rewards are part of the system. Food is the classic reward, and often the most practical. Remember that the reward is a training tool — once the behavior is established, you no longer need to dish out treats for each successful action.

In addition to food, the most effective rewards to use are: toys and play, praise, and affection.

Toys need not be complicated or expensive: cats go crazy for scrunched up bits of paper, cardboard boxes or twigs and feathers, which can be picked up for free on your next walk near a park.

Praising your cat usually sounds something like "Good job, Jasper!" or "Good boy!"; it's the warm and enthusiastic tone of voice that will really make your cat know you're delighted. Affection means petting, patting or stroking your cat in a way you know he really likes. Fluffy Boy really loves chin scratches, as well as getting scratched along his jawline or behind the ears, whereas another cat I have, Quincey, loves shoulder pats: pat-pat left, pat-pat right, and so on.

While rewards are no longer strictly necessary once the behavior is entrenched, it remains a delight to dole out praise or physical affection when your cat has done what you wanted her to. It's a pleasure for both of you.

Using food as a reward

Food is the most practical training reward, because it's quick: You click, give the treat, your cat downs the treat, and you can repeat. Rewards that involve physical activity (especially playing with toys) take longer and can hinder the momentum of your training session. They may also serve as a distraction.

When it comes to choosing food treats, deliciousness and hoovering speed are important. Fresh food, such as roast chicken, ham or cheese, cut up into pea-sized bits, are more typically more flavorful than commercial treats. Being soft, they are also quicker to down. Speed is good when you want your cat to connect the dots, instead of getting distracted by a whole lot of chewing.

Whatever the reward, remember that you only give one when you were shown the behavior you were after. If you call your cat and it only comes on the fifth call, that's no treat.

Consider your cat's daily food intake. Training food should come broadly out of your cat's daily energy intake. There's no need to break out a calculator and calorimeter, but let common sense guide you.

Cats on special diets might not be able to have cheese, ham and so forth — use their special food as treats instead. Even cats on special diets are likely to be able to have plain boiled chicken breast. Check with your vet if in doubt.

Some people worry about relying on food for desired behavior to the extent that a cat might put on weight, but once a behavior is established, you can offer food as an occasional reward — an actual treat.

Building duration and distance with behaviors

As with any training, the goal in clicker training is to establish certain behaviors and ensure their reliable performance. Duration is the length of time the animal can maintain the desired behavior, and distance is your physical distance from the animal.

By building duration and distance we mean being able to maintain the behaviors for longer (for example, sitting and staying nicely on the cat tree until Mom has finished chopping the vegetables and cooking the spaghetti), and responding to cues even when we are further away.

In training, expect your cat to find duration challenging. For some actions, such as "come," duration is irrelevant, but in holding positions (for example "stay") the longer the hold, the greater the challenge.

It is important to realize you need to help your cat to build up duration over days, weeks and even months. Think back to when you were five years old. Could you sit still for half an hour just because your mother asked you to, or was it an ability you built up over time?

Distance, too, is a factor in training. The further, physically, you are from your cat, the more difficult it is to influence him. Start by training in close physical proximity, and move away slowly, over many sessions.

Examples of behaviors that can be taught using duration and distance

In dog training, duration and distance are a major consideration; in cat training less so, although they do come into play. In duration, especially, cats have an edge over dogs, as by nature they keep still for long stretches of time. (Consider what a cat looks like when it's hunting: it can keep dead still for ages observing its prey.)

In our training, it's more a matter of wanting the cat to keep still, but where we want her to keep still — for example, up on her cat tree, or on a specific stool instead of on the dining table or between the kettle and stovetop.

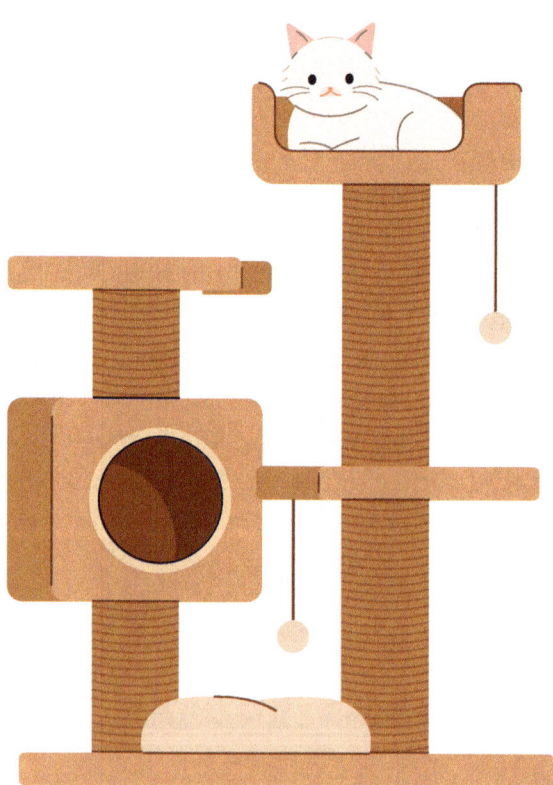

TIPS FOR BUILDING DURATION AND DISTANCE EFFECTIVELY AND MAINTAINING PROGRESS

- Build up slowly. Aim for an initial "stay" of three seconds, then another five.
- In a second session, you could build up to a stay of fifteen seconds. If the cat jumps off, start again, luring with the target, clicking for the stay, and treating after three seconds.
- Occasionally, after a long hold with click and treat, repeat the click and treat after just three seconds again. This comes as a welcome surprise and boosts motivation.
- Always keep things easy for your cat. Don't set the benchmark too high, because that sets you up for failure.
- Begin in close physical proximity to your cat, and move away slowly over many sessions.
- Once your cat has established a successful "stay" with you beside him, in the next session, work on having him stay as you move around the room (as you would in real life, where you would be cooking dinner or building your model airplane.)

Tips for successful training sessions and maintaining progress

TIPS FOR STRUCTURING SUCCESSFUL TRAINING SESSIONS

- Start with a hungry cat. If you free-feed your cat, take the food bowl away for three hours before training.
- Get distractions out of the way. This includes people and other pets.
- Unlike your cat, it might be good for you to have a snack before you start. You don't want to be hangry.
- Err on the side of too short and too easy.
- Plan ahead: What is it that you, in real life, want from this training? For example, you might want your cat to be able to follow a target to get out from a hiding spot under the bed when you need to take her to the vet, or the carpet cleaners are approaching with the vacuum cleaner.

STRATEGIES FOR MAINTAINING PROGRESS AND AVOIDING SETBACKS

- This can't be overstated: be accurate with your timing. If you're training your cat to wait patiently for her dinner, but she starts mewing for it and you click on the mew, you're reinforcing the operatics, not the sitting.
- Remember shaping: When your cat is doing well, keep raising the bar. For example, if she's easily following the target, make it more challenging by moving a little further.
- Celebrate the small victories instead of just focusing on the final, far-off result.

TIPS FOR TROUBLESHOOTING COMMON PROBLEMS AND SETBACKS IN TRAINING

- If the behavior deteriorates (usually because you've become sloppy about when you click, i.e. what you're reinforcing) just go back to basics. You've got this.
- If a behavior is just not coming together, you're probably consistently clicking too late. Ask a friend to watch or record you to check.
- Remember that training is communication. What you click and reward is what you are telling your cat you want — and it will be repeated. If you want your cat off the table but click before she jumps, instead of when she's landing on the ground, you're reinforcing being on the table.

BASIC COMMANDS

FOUNDATIONAL COMMANDS

TARGET TOUCH

Easy

Teaching commands with movement come before commands to sit or stay still, so the first one we teach is "come." In reality, "touch target" is the first version of "come" we teach. This foundational command has many practical applications: leading your cat in and out of his carrier, out from under the bed, or getting him to jump off furniture (or on, for performing tricks).

Materials:
- Treats
- Clicker
- Target stick: a wooden spoon, pencil, stick or chopstick

Hand Signal:
A rolling motion with one hand.

Step-by-step:

1. Begin the session by reinforcing click = treat ("charging the clicker"): click and give a treat at the same moment. Your cat is likely to realize you're onto a good thing here.

2. Repeat the "charge up" a handful of times. Click and treat simultaneously the first few times, then click and, after a delay of a second or two, give the treat. Always click first, treat after.

3. Hold the target stick about three inches in front of your cat's nose. Cats are naturally inquisitive and like to make sense of things by smelling them, so your cat is likely to touch her nose to the target. Excellent! Click at the moment of touch, move the target out of sight, then treat. Repeat several times to reinforce.

4. A touch or bump to the target scores a click, scores a treat.

Basic Training Techniques

5. After the cat has successfully touched or bumped the target up close a few times, and you've clicked and rewarded accordingly, start moving the target a little further away. This way, your cat must actively step forward to get to the target. (See the tip below.)

6. Once your cat has learned to step up to the target when you've moved it an inch or two away, you can proceed to move it a foot or two, until your cat learns to follow the target as you move it along.

Key Elements/Things to keep in mind: It aids the learning process if your cat hears the click while she is moving, because she realizes that the click was indeed the result of something she did, and not a random thing.

If your cat doesn't seem interested in the target, rub a little food on the tip, and that should pique their interest. Also, instead of holding it out a couple of inches, bring the target close to your cat's nose, so that they almost have to touch it.

NAME RECOGNITION

Easy

Getting your cat to recognize and respond to its name is important for bonding. It's also a precursor step to "come."

Materials:
- Treats
- Clicker

Hand Signal: None

Step-by-step:

1. As always, begin with a hungry cat in a room free of distractions or other animals.

2. Clicker at the ready, say your cat's name. She's likely to look your way, or even just turn her ears towards you just at the sound of your voice. At the moment she turns her head (or even just her ears) click and treat.

3. If she ignores you, just do nothing. Wait a few moments and try again.

4. Once she has successfully looked your way three of four times on hearing her name (reinforced, each time with a click and treat), say a random word or name. Now, if she looks your way, do nothing. The point is to reinforce her reaction when you say her own name only.

5. Repeat steps 2 through 4 until your cat loses interest, indicating an end to the training session.

Key Elements/Things to keep in mind: Keeping other animals out of the room for this training avoids the confusion of other animals responding to your voice.

You could help the learning by putting a unique "tune" or tonal pattern to your cat's name, which you would use each time you call them. For example, long-short: "Luuuuu-cy," or a low-high tone: low on "Lu" and high on "cy," for example.

COME RECALL

Easy

Teaching your cat to come has obvious practical advantages, but it's also important for your cat's safety. Say your cat slips out of the apartment and gets lost in the building, or darts into the neighbor's yard, a successful recall cue can save you and your cat hours of distress. The recall is different from just the ordinary "here, kitty, kitty" (using their name from across the room). It's used for when you need your cat by your side right away.

Materials:
- Treats
- Clicker

Hand Signal: None, but you will use a sound cue, such as rapping your knuckles on a hard surface.

Step-by-step:

1. Think of the sound cue you will use to call your cat, instead of using the word "come" or calling by name. (See the tip below.) Make sure your sound is different from a knock on the door, because that would confuse the cat, and cause it to dart to the door whenever someone comes.

2. While you will still be using the clicker method for the recall, in this case you begin with the rap/tap sound.

3. The principle remains the same: we summon the cat (rap), click when it starts moving toward us and reward it with a treat to reinforce the behavior.

4. Double tap your knuckles on a hard surface to make the "rap/tap" sound.

5. Wait for your cat to come to your hand holding the treat.

6. Reward the cat with the treat immediately once they come.

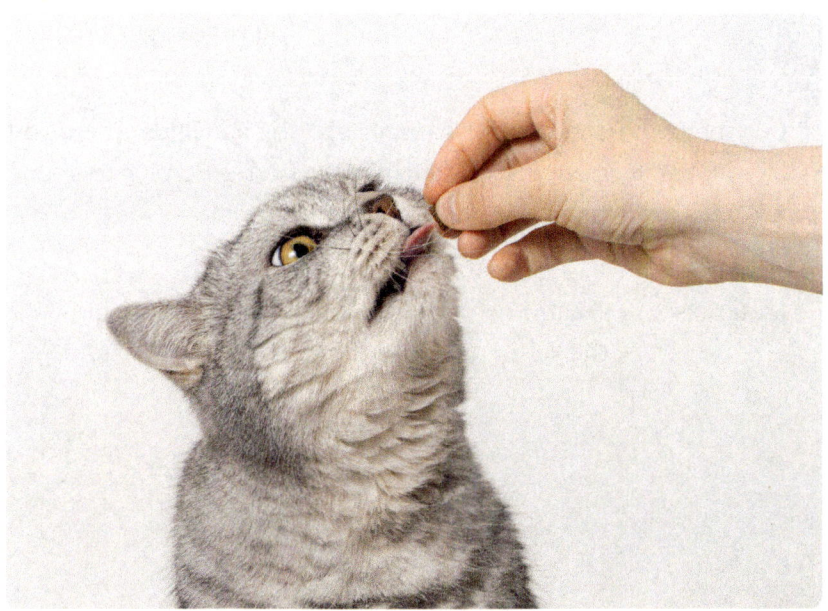

Whereas in target touching we are creating a new behavior and shaping it, with the recall we are taking an existing behavior, but ensuring a reliable, consistent response to our signal.

Always reward a successful recall immediately. Don't, however, reward if your cat initially ignores you. What you reward, persists. If you provide a treat when the cat comes only on your third or fourth call, you are training him to come only on a third or fourth call.

In other words, cat comes on first call: treat. Cat ignores you, and saunters along on the fifth call, ignore cat back. No cussing, no fussing, just an ignore for an ignore. And note, that's not to be spiteful, it's just to avoid reinforcing unwanted behavior!

Key Elements/Things to keep in mind: If you already have a dog who readily comes to you when you use the word "come," you may want to use a cat-specific sound instead. This will avoid a stampede of dog(s) and cat(s) rushing at you all at once. For cats, many trainers like to use a double tap of the knuckles on the nearest hard surface as their recall cue.

SIT

Easy*

"Sit" is the precursor to "stay" as well as all the activities where you need your cat to sit still in a relaxed manner, from grooming to sitting on the vet's exam table.

Materials:
- Treats
- Clicker

Hand Signal: Open palm facing downwards, single downward motion as you say "sit."

_____

* May take extra patience

Step-by-step:

1. Begin with a cat that is naturally standing or walking about anywhere you're happy for your cat to sit. (If you start off with a cat that is already sitting, it might be at least half asleep, which is no good for training.)

2. The floor is a good place to start. If you're not comfortable on the floor yourself, take a seat on a low stool or sofa nearby.

3. Be patient. Very patient. Wait until your cat sits down of his own accord. Immediately click, then treat.

4. If your cat stays seated, click and treat two or three more times.

5. If your cat gets up to take the treat, wait for him to sit down before the next click. This is where you might need extra patience: it could take a cat quite some time (over numerous sessions) to realize what exactly is being rewarded here.

6. Once the cat starts voluntarily sitting down again after taking the treat (possibly not in your first training session for this behavior), introduce your hand signal, saying the cue word, "Sit," at the same time.

7. Click and treat for sitting down on cue, but no longer for sitting down that happens without the cue word/signal.

Key Elements/Things to keep in mind: While this is an easy behavior to teach, it's not the one to start with! Remember to start your training with the active commands of "target touch" and "come."

STAY

Intermediate*

Very useful for creating calm and order around feeding time or when you're working in the kitchen.

Materials:

- Treats
- Clicker
- Mat station, high chair or cat tree

Hand Signal:

For "stay": Arm out straight in front of you with wrist flexed so palm is facing the wall in front of you.

For "up" (to the cat tree or a high chair): Point up at the object.

* Be sure to master "sit" first.

Step-by-step:

1. Teach sit and stay only once touch target and recall ("come") are well established. Get your clicker, treats and hungry cat lined up.

2. Choose a spot that (a) is safely out of the way and (b) the cat will like. You might choose a high chair, or your cat's cat tree or mat station.

3. Entice your cat to the spot either by leading it with your target (like a magic wand!) or by placing a treat where you want it to go.

4. Click as it jumps up, and then give another treat. Silently count to three. If the cat is still seated, click and treat again.

5. Keep this going. Once the cat has finished its treat, if it is still sitting, count a few more seconds this time, then click and treat again.

6. Once the behavior is established, and the cat is doing it spontaneously for clicks, you can add in the spoken cue: "Up!" or "Stay!" (with the appropriate hand signal) when you want your cat to take his place.

Key Elements/Things to keep in mind: Our hand signals are suggestions only, and you can always make up your own. To avoid confusing your cat, keep each hand signal to its own command, and don't use two signals that are too alike.

LIE DOWN

Intermediate*

Useful in grooming and at the vet, and a precursor to "no biting" during play.

Materials:

- Treats
- Clicker
- Target stick
- Mat station, high perch or any place your cat is already comfortable with lying down.

Hand Signal:

Hand straight out, palm down, and bend the wrist down in a double patting motion.

Step-by-step:

1. Begin, as always in a quiet, distraction-free room, with your clicker and treats handy.

2. Place a treat on your cat's mat station, or wherever you would like it to lie down. Many cats might initially feel unsafe lying on the floor, as this is a vulnerable position. If your cat is most content lying down on your bed or its own cat tree, start there.

3. Give the "sit" cue.

4. Once your cat is sitting, lure her into the down position using your target stick. Begin with the target close to her nose, and bring it to the floor/bed/mat station/other surface.

5. Click and treat for any movement in the desired direction: bending elbows, nose down, or side of the head down.

---

* To be trained after "sit" and "stay" have been mastered.

6 Keep going (over as many repetitions or sessions as it takes) until your cat is lying down. Click and treat.

7 Keep going. Once the cat has finished its treat, if it is still lying down, count a few more seconds this time, then click and treat again.

8 Once the behavior is established, and the cat is doing it spontaneously for clicks, you can add your spoken cue: "Lie down," with the hand signal.

Key Elements/Things to keep in mind: Once your cat does the action on cue, it's important to stop clicking for the action happening not on cue. Otherwise your cat might expect to get a click/treat every single time he does the action.

Bonus tip: This action might be easier to teach with your cat up on a perch, such as the cat tree. This enables you to lower your wand an inch or two below the cat's own level, making it easier for them to follow into a lying position.

BASIC COMMANDS

SKILL LEARNING

WEARING A HARNESS

Easy

This is the precursor to leash walking. Being comfortable in a harness is also helpful for traveling or on vet visits, when the harness gives you something safe to grab onto in an emergency — for example, your cat gets spooked and tries to wriggle from your grip into the traffic, or into the jaws of the big, panicked dog in the waiting room.

Materials:
- Cat harness
- Treats
- Clicker

Hand Signal: None

Step-by-step:

1. Begin with a soft harness, the sort made especially for cats. Adjust it to your best estimate for a loose yet secure fit on your cat.

2. Leave it around for a while so that your cat can sniff and explore it.

3. After a day or so, slip the harness onto your cat.

4. Simply leave the cat to go about the house with the harness on for periods of fifteen minutes at a time.

Key Elements/Things to keep in mind: Feel free to click and treat when you see the cat sniffing the harness, or later, walking around in it without a fuss.

Basic Training Techniques

WALKING ON A LEASH

Intermediate

While few cats will want to go on walks the way dogs do, cats can be trained to be happy on a leash. Leash walks are a great way for cats to safely do some outdoor exploring without the danger of cars, other cats, coyotes or raccoons — and without your cat harming birds, mice or other wildlife.

Materials:
- Cat harness
- Cat leash
- Treats
- Clicker

Hand Signal: None

Step-by-step:

1. Once your cat is used to the harness, clip a light cat leash onto it and let your cat do their own thing, indoors. This will accustom them to the harness and leash combination. The leash will get stuck on furniture. Don't make a fuss: just calmly untangle it each time and let your cat carry on wandering about the house for about fifteen minutes at a time.

2. Repeat over several days. Only once your cat is comfortable dragging around the leash can you go outside.

3. On getting outside, simply hold the end of the leash and let your cat explore. If she explores, follow, but if she just hovers or stares, let her. She's just getting used to the sights and sounds of the great outdoors.

4. Continue in this way over several sessions, and eventually your cat will be perfectly happy exploring with you on the other end of the leash. It's a very different system to dog-walking, where the human is the leader! And that's totally okay: the goal isn't to go on great big hikes, but for your cat to

safely do a little outdoor exploring, wiggle her toes in the grass, and broaden her horizons.

Key Elements/Things to keep in mind: Once your cat is comfortable, you can use the clicker and treats to encourage her to walk on a few steps.

MAT STATION

Intermediate

A useful alternative to "stay" in which your cat goes to a specific spot, whether a specific cat mat or cat bed.

Materials:

- Treats
- Clicker
- Target stick
- Mat station (your cat's dining place mat or other cat mat) or cat bed

Hand Signal:

Closed fist moved in a single downward motion (like "rock" in the game rock, paper, scissors) as you say "mat" or "on your bed."

Step-by-step:

1. Ensure you and your cat have already mastered "sit" and "stay."

2. Begin a few feet away from your cat's mat (or cat bed).

3. With the target stick, lure your cat to the mat station.

4. Now, using your hand signal for "sit," get your cat to sit. Click and treat.

5. Go back to your starting point a few feet away, and using your cat's name, get her to join you at the starting point.

6. After several repetitions or sessions, once the cat is offering the behavior freely, start adding the new cue with hand signal. Reinforce the connection between the action and new cue through repetition.

7. Finally, click and treat for sitting down on the mat station/cat bed on cue only, and no longer for sitting down that happens without the cue.

Key Elements/Things to keep in mind: This is an extension of "sit" and "stay" and it may take your cat time to realize what you want from him, namely, that he should (1) go to a specific point (2) sit down there and (3) stay.

Basic Training Techniques

BRUSHING

Easy

Having a cat that tolerates brushing is important for hygiene and general maintenance. Some cats' fur will mat when not brushed regularly, and this can be painful or create a breeding ground for parasites. The benefit of brushing excess hair from the coat of a shedding coat is obvious, but also, it is when we groom our animals that we get to notice any injuries, wounds, ticks or fleas we might otherwise note have discovered. Brushing your cat is also a very enjoyable bonding exercise for both of you, once your cat is willing to relax into it.

Materials:
- Treats
- Clicker (or use tongue clicks)
- Cat brush

Hand Signal: None

Step-by-step:

1. Get your cat used to getting handled in general, if they are not yet already. Many cats are happy getting touched, but not always in all places. And some cats aren't sure about getting picked up in the first place, so begin with picking up.

2. Be gentle. Use both hands: one at the back and the other at the front, and support the legs using an arm.

3. If your cat is resistant to getting picked up, over the course of a few days, pick him up and click-treat at the smallest sign of relaxing.

4. Once things are going well, you can add a cue, like "up-up!" before gently picking them up.

5. To get going with brushing, begin in a relaxed setting where your cat already likes to sit, for example the TV couch. Don't force him to sit in your lap if he doesn't like that. Simply brush him lightly, along the back and neck. Click at signs of relaxation or enjoyment.

6. During this process, if you don't know them already, find the spots your cat loves to be stroked or scratched. Favorite spots tend to be along the jawline, the back of the head or neck, behind the ears and at the base of the tail. Your hands will be busy, so you can use tongue clicks here: stroke or scratch the liked spots, and click at the sign of enjoyment.

7. When you discover a spot your cat does not like being touched, back away, and right away get back to a spot they do like. Tongue click.

8. Keep going in this way. Once your cat is relaxed, gently handle a disliked area for a short moment, and immediately move to a liked area.

9. Once your cat eases into being handled, click at the first sign of relaxing, say, the paw it didn't like touched before. Praise, and release the pressure of the touch at the same moment.

10. Eventually you will be able to brush your cat all over without a fuss.

Key Elements/Things to keep in mind: It's important for your cat to feel relaxed being touched on every part of the body, for the sake of health-checks and vet care. Your cat might not love getting touched on her tummy initially, but if you get her used to it, and she ever gets a wound to the belly — or even a mat that needs shaving off — you'll be grateful for your training.

Step 9, above, teaches your cat that the very act of relaxing its muscles makes you back off touching a disliked area. This is another example of how training works when your cat feels they have buy-in.

NAIL TRIMMING

Intermediate to advanced*

Trimmed nails mean fewer snags to clothing and furniture.

Materials:
- Treats
- Clicker (or use tongue clicks)
- Cat nail clipper

Hand Signal: None

---

* Depending on the cat. Ensure you have completed the brushing training before attempting nails.

Step-by-step:

1. Before your first home nail trim, ask your groomer or vet to show you how to safely trim a cat's nails; it's important not to cut them too short.

2. Ensure your nail clipper is specifically designed for cats. Don't use human or dog nail clippers on your cat.

3. Begin, without the clippers, in a relaxed setting, for example when your cat is snuggled on your lap or beside you during TV time. Ever so gently stroke his paws. Click for signs of relaxation.

4. If your cat really isn't into it, and jumps up and leaves, let him. You'll try again in another session.

5. Alternate touching the paws with scratching or petting favored areas, such as under the chin.

6. Repeating these steps, very gently get your cat accustomed to different types of paw touch: light pressure or stroking to the top of the paw, the underside, the feeling of having the toes gently splayed, and very light massage to the webbing.

7. Finally, when your cat is completely relaxed having his paws touched, you will be able to clip his nails without resistance.

Key Elements/Things to keep in mind: Most cats feel very vulnerable and exposed lying on their backs, so don't force that. Sphinx position, with the paw getting groomed gently lifted, is a great posture for nail trimming.

TEETH BRUSHING

Advanced

Your vet might recommend brushing your cat's teeth to prevent tooth and gum disease.

Materials:
- Treats
- Clicker (or use tongue clicks)
- Soft cat toothbrush
- Toothpaste for cats

Hand Signal: None

Step-by-step:

1. Ensure your toothbrush and toothpaste are specifically designed for cats. Don't use human or dog toothpaste or toothbrushes.

2. First set toothbrush and toothpaste aside, and simply get your cat relaxed with having his mouth opened. Begin, again, in a relaxed setting, by simply playing with your cat's lips, gently moving them up and down, or lightly massaging them.

3. Follow the pointers in "Brushing" and "Nail trimming" in getting your cat comfortable with getting these sensitive areas handled.

4. Finally — and this might take many sessions — your cat will let you lift his lips to expose the teeth. Now, as gently as in the previous steps, get her used to the feeling of the bristles on her teeth, without toothpaste.

5. Finally, when she's okay with having her lips and gums massaged, and with the feeling of the bristles, add the toothpaste to the equation. Let her sniff it: cat toothpaste comes in flavors like beef and chicken, so she should be enticed.

6. Cat toothpaste is designed to swallow, so there's no rinsing to worry about!

Key Elements/Things to keep in mind: With the physical, or handling, skills, you get to use gentle touch as a reinforcer, instead of food.

EAR CLEANING

Intermediate to advanced*

Most cats do a good job of cleaning their own ears, but if your cat is prone to ear infections, your vet might instruct you to clean your cat's ears at home. Overcleaning can itself lead to ear infections, so follow your vet's advice.

Materials:
- Treats
- Clicker (or use tongue clicks)
- Vet-recommended ear-cleaning solution for cats
- Cotton balls or gauze

Hand Signal: None

Step-by-step:

1. Only ever use a vet-recommended ear-cleaning product.
2. First simply get your cat used to having her ears touched, stroked, and gently flapped back.
3. Follow the pointers in "Brushing" and "Nail trimming" in getting your cat comfortable with getting these sensitive areas handled.
4. Once — after several sessions — your cat will let you manipulate her ears, you're ready. First pull the ears slightly back and inspect them. Then drip the prescribed amount of cleaning solution into the cat's first ear. Gently massage the base of the ear using your forefinger and thumb for about half a minute. When you let go, she'll want to shake her head. Let her.
5. Repeat on the other side.
6. Take your cotton balls, and pat or blot the ears dry inside.

Key Elements/Things to keep in mind: Never use cotton-on-a-stick-type swabs to clean your cat's ears, as this can push wax or other debris into the ear canal.

CHAPTER 4
ADVANCED COMMANDS

Now that you and your cat have a solid foundation, it's time to build on those basics with even more engaging and impressive tricks. Having worked through the fundamentals, your cat has developed a strong grasp on following cues and associating actions with rewards. Now, you'll deepen that training with commands that tap into their natural curiosity and playfulness, creating a more dynamic and responsive learning experience.

These advanced tricks—like "Spin," "Jump," and "High Five"—are designed to challenge your cat's agility and enthusiasm in new ways. By continuing to reinforce their progress, you'll see your cat grow more confident and eager to interact. Each new command is an opportunity to explore your cat's abilities and strengthen the unique connection you've developed through training.

TRICK TRAINING

SPIN

Easy

This is a fun trick to show off to your friends.

Materials:
- Treats
- Clicker
- Target stick or toy on a piece of string

Hand Signal:
A stirring motion with the index finger pointed.

Step-by-step:

1. Begin with a calm, sufficiently hungry cat, as always. Cut your treats into smaller bits as you will be training in small increments.

2. Train for quarter revolutions first. Using your lure (target stick or toy dangling from string), lead your cat into turning a quarter revolution. Click, treat and repeat, until you have a full revolution.

3. Next, add more revolutions simply by guiding the cat with your lure.

4. To add the cue, hold up the lure, and when you see the cat is about to give you the behavior (spin in a circle) add your hand signal and the voice cue: "Spin!"

5. Keep going (maybe in this session, or maybe in a following session). Now click only for spins where you've given the cue. For spins without the cue, don't click.

Key Elements/Things to keep in mind: Don't go overboard with speed. You're not trying to make your cat dizzy! (If she makes herself dizzy on her own time, when she gets the zoomies, that's her business.)

JUMP

Easy

This can be used as an intro to agility training, but also as a precursor to "sit" and "stay" (Chapter 3). You can also use it to get your cat up onto places you would like it to go, such as the cat tree.

Materials:

- Treats
- Clicker
- Target stick
- A surface or object for the cat to jump onto, e.g. a chair

Hand Signal:

A sweeping motion with the hand from your mid-thigh to shoulder.

Step-by-step:

1. Begin with your cat seated or standing near the object he will be jumping onto. Move the lure from close to his nose, up onto the object. He is very likely to follow.

2. If your cat does not follow, stop, pause, and go again.

3. Once you've had a successful jump, click and treat.

4. Repeat, adding your cue (hand signal and the word, "jump,"). Now only click jumps that follow the cue — avoid clicking random jumps.

Key Elements/Things to keep in mind: Only train with objects or surfaces that you are actually happy for your cat to be jumping onto.

JUMP ADVANCED (INTO YOUR ARMS)

Intermediate to advanced

This is a very cute trick, but, like recall, may be used to get your cat to safety/a more comfortable position quickly.

Materials:

- Treats
- Clicker
- Target stick
- A friend or family member as co-trainer
- A thick sweatshirt (that you don't mind getting snagged)

Hand Signal:

Pat both hands on the chest, under the collar bones. (Then hold arms out for cat to land on.)

Step-by-step:

1. Once "Jump" is established, you can start training this one. Begin with your cat on the floor, or on the furniture. You're wearing the sweatshirt (in case your cat brings out its claws for holding on.) Your co-trainer — someone your cat is well familiar and comfortable with — is holding the target stick in one hand and treats in the other, because you have only two hands!

2. Kneel on the floor, or crouch, clicker in one hand. Your arms shouldn't be too far off the ground. The idea is to make the first jumps super easy.

3. Your co-trainer holds out the lure, placing it close to the cat's nose. Now he or she trails the lure up your arms.

4. This is likely totally new for your cat, so it might take several attempts, or several sessions. Click and treat movement in the right direction, such as the cat placing its paws on your wrists.

Advanced Commands

5. Finally, once your cat is actually jumping onto your arms at will, add the cue: Using the hand signal, pat your chest, then quickly cross your arms to make a secure landing space. It might take many repetitions and lots of patience to get here. By this point, the target stick will no longer be necessary.

6. Later, once your cat reliably performs this trick, you can slowly make the jumping distance higher by coming out of the crouch/kneeling position.

Key Elements/Things to keep in mind: Once you've successfully trained this move, you can advance to a "gentle-paws" version. No longer click jumps where the claws come out, but only jumps that are both on cue AND with claws retracted, until finally you can safely do this trick in short sleeves.

Tip 2: Ensuring you've trained the click well is very important here, otherwise you might find your cat trying to jump up onto you at random times, expecting to be rewarded!

> **HIGH FIVE**

Intermediate

This cute trick is a fun bonding exercise (as are most of the tricks in this chapter).

Materials:
- Treats
- Clicker
- Target stick

Hand Signal:
Hand up in high-five position.

Step-by-step:

1. Begin seated beside your cat. The first goal is to get your cat to raise her paw.

2. Hover the target stick an inch or so above the ground, near your cat's paw. She is likely to want to swat the stick. Ignore energetic swats, but click and reward gentle taps.

3. Progress until the paw is higher off the ground. Now click and reward only for taps high off the ground.

4. Replace the target stick with just your hand, in high-five position (wrist flexed) but hand still relatively low to the ground. Raise your hand in increments during the training.

5. Don't click and reward taps with claws out. Ignore, but do click gentle taps.

6. Once your cat is giving you the high five, introduce your hand signal with the spoken cue, "high-five" and now click for only high fives on cue.

Key Elements/Things to keep in mind: The way our instructions are written, it might seem the steps are a recipe to follow from beginning to end in each session. This is not necessarily the case: let your cat guide you. When she's had enough, quit until the opportunity for the next session arrives.

ROLL OVER

Intermediate

A cute and playful move.

Materials:
- Treats
- Clicker
- Target stick

Hand Signal:
A rolling motion with one hand.

Step-by-step:

1. Begin with your cat lying on his side. Using your lure (target stick), lead your cat into turning a quarter revolution or more, depending on what your cat will give you. Click, treat and repeat, until you have a full revolution.

2. Next, add more revolutions simply by guiding the cat with your lure.

3. To add the cue, hold up the lure, and when you see the cat is about to give you a full rollover, add your hand signal and the voice cue: "Roll over!"

4. Keep going. Now click only for spins where you've given the cue. For rollovers without the cue, don't click.

Key Elements/Things to keep in mind: Your cat will let you know when any given training session is over. This is not stubbornness, but a function of the cat's attention span when it comes to focused learning.

Easy

A sweet party trick.

Materials:

- Treats
- Clicker
- Target stick

Hand Signal:

Wave

Step-by-step:

1. Begin seated beside your cat. As with High Five, the first goal is to get her to raise her paw.

2. Bring her paw higher with repetition, in a similar procedure as with High Five, but without her touching your hand.

3. Progress until the paw is higher off the ground, and now start training the back-and-forth motion of the wave by using a back-and-forth motion of the target stick.

4. Initially your cat might want to follow the movement of the target stick with her hand instead of her paw, or she might try to swat the target. Again, don't worry — just click the desired actions, and ignore the rest. Be patient.

5. Once your cat waves spontaneously, introduce your hand signal with the spoken cue, "wave" and now click for only waves on cue.

Key Elements/Things to keep in mind: Even tricks and behaviors that are classified as "easy" might take lots of time and repetition to teach. Don't give up.

Easy to intermediate

A useful complement to "sit" and "stay."

Materials:

- Treats
- Clicker
- Target stick
- A perch for the cat to jump onto, e.g. a high chair or cat tree

Hand Signal:

Point at the perch with a double flick of the wrist.

Step-by-step:

1. The steps are very similar to "Jump": Begin with your cat seated or standing near the perch. Move the lure from close to his nose, up onto the perch.

2. If your cat does not follow, stop, pause, and go again.

3. Once you've had a successful jump to perch, click and treat.

4. Repeat, adding your cue (hand signal and the word, "perch,"). Now only click jumps that follow the cue — avoid clicking random jumps.

5. Add the element of "stay" by rewarding stays of longer and longer periods, from three seconds up.

Key Elements/Things to keep in mind: If you have a boisterous dog, and a cat that likes to hang out by the door, you could train your cat to "go to perch" before letting the dog back in from potty break to keep them out of each other's way.

KISSES

Intermediate

Nothing but cute! This will take a little training to get the cat out of licking or sniffing your face and into simply pressing its nose to your cheek.

Materials:

- Treats
- Clicker
- Tiny bits of butter, yoghurt or peanut butter

Hand Signal: None.

Step-by-step:

1. Dab a tiny bit of the food on each of your cheeks, or the tip of your nose or your forehead.

2. Sit on the floor beside your cat and present your face. Your cat will lick at the food. Don't click yet, or you'll just be training your cat to lick your face.

3. Wait until the licking stops, and your cat is sniffing at your face, or pressing its nose against you. Click and reward nose presses.

4. Once you reliably get nose presses (or gentle head-butts to the side of your face, if you want), start training with your cue word: "Kisses!"

Key Elements/Things to keep in mind: Most cats don't love being cornered, so don't be surprised if your cat doesn't want to throw being hugged into the equation.

SPEAK

Easy

Most people are going to want to train their cats to be less vocal, but getting them to pipe up on cue can be very cute. This is very easy to train, but you need to be astute enough to catch the vocalizations as they happen.

Materials:
- Treats
- Clicker

Hand Signal: None.

Step-by-step:

1. Wait until your cat gives you the kind of meow or chirrup you'd like to hear more of. Click and treat. If your cat makes sounds you don't want to hear more of, just ignore them.

2. Once the sound comes up more frequently, watch and listen carefully so you can pre-empt the sound. Use your cue word just before you can tell you're going to hear the sound, then click and reward.

3. Now click and reward only when the sound is made on cue.

Key Elements/Things to keep in mind: This trick is best taught on the fly. Carry your clicker and treats in your pocket, and when you cat makes the kind of sounds you'd like to hear more of, follow the steps above.

CHAPTER 5

CLICKER TRAINING FOR PROBLEM BEHAVIOR CORRECTION

Clicker training is uniquely effective for behavior modification because it builds on positive reinforcement rather than punishment or correction. When addressing problem behaviors, it's easy to focus on what we want our cat to stop doing—scratching furniture, jumping on counters, or biting, for example. However, simply trying to curb an unwanted behavior without providing an alternative often leads to frustration for both the cat and owner. Clicker training offers a solution by shifting the focus to rewarding desired behaviors, which encourages your cat to naturally choose these over problematic ones.

The success of clicker training in behavior modification lies in its clarity. Each click marks the exact moment your cat performs a behavior you want to reinforce, making it easy for them to understand what's expected. This method is particularly beneficial for cats, who tend to be independent and may react negatively to traditional training methods that rely on discipline. With the clicker, there's no confusion or intimidation—just a clear signal that lets your cat know they're on the right track. Over time, this consistent reinforcement shapes their habits and gradually reduces undesirable actions.

BEHAVIOR MODIFICATION

CALMING ANXIETY (PETS, PICKED UP, HIDING)

Easy to intermediate*

Your cat may be anxious or skittish for a variety of reasons, including insufficient socialization in kittenhood, or negative experiences with other humans. Positive reinforcement and clicker training can go a long way in calming an anxious cat. Goals would include getting your cat to allow you to pick them up, and a reduction in anxious hiding.

Materials:

- Treats
- Clicker
- Target stick, if you like

Hand Signal:

None.

Step-by-step:

1. Begin any moment, anywhere you see the opportunity to do some calm positive reinforcement of desired behavior, in other words, whenever your cat looks a little less skittish.

2. Click and treat for any movement in a positive direction: your cat coming a step closer to you, allowing you a step closer, allowing someone new to get closer, etc.

3. If using the target stick, use it to draw your cat closer to you. Click and treat for any movement towards you.

4. Repeat, repeat and repeat over days, weeks or months, if necessary, whenever the opportunity presents itself.

Key Elements/Things to keep in mind: Here's where you can use your training with the target stick to really work for you: Use the target to lure your cat out from under beds, off of high perches, and closer to you.

---

* Depending on the cat.

SCRATCHING

Easy to intermediate

The usefulness of this one is obvious! Who would want their furniture, priceless antique rugs, curtains and even walls scratched to smithereens when you could train your cat to let rip on an array of scratch posts instead?

Materials:

- Treats
- Clicker
- Solid, upright scratch post
- Catnip, if your cat's into that
- Target stick, if you want

Hand Signal:

None.

Step-by-step:

1. Begin by placing the scratch post in what is, from the cat's perspective, an ideal place to mark:
   - Prominent position in the room,
   - Upright and vertical,
   - Solid and secure (so your cat can put his back into it without the post toppling over),
   - A texture that lets the claws sink in, while being soft enough to leave shred marks (because visual marking of territory is the whole point).

2. Allow your cat to investigate the scratch post — you could use your target stick to lure them to it.

3. Click and reward your cat sniffing at the post or rubbing their face against it.

4. Click and reward any actual scratching.

5. Repeat steps 2 — 4 as often as necessary, over as many days and weeks as necessary.

6. To attract your cat to the post, sprinkle some catnip on it if your cat likes catnip.

7. It's a good idea to add a scratch post to each room your cat spends time in. Repeat the above steps with each new scratch post.

Key Elements/Things to keep in mind: Scratching is natural and necessary behavior for cats. It's not something you can stop, but you can redirect it, and that's the key.

COUNTER SURFIING

Easy*

Nobody likes cat hair on their PB & J, and nobody wants to have their cat sticking his face into their cereal bowl. Cats sure love counter surfing, but you can train them out of it.

Materials:

- Treats
- Clicker
- Target stick

Hand Signal:

None.

---

* Can only be done once Target Touch is successfully established.

Step-by-step:

1. Have your clicker and treats at the ready, because this is a behavior you need to train on the fly.

2. When your cat hops onto the counter, lure her off with your target stick.

3. Click and reward as she lands on the ground.

4. If, or when, your cat jumps on the counter again, do not scold, physically put them on the floor or push them in any direction. Simply use the lure, and when you get the desired jump onto the ground, click and treat.

5. Repeat over days, weeks and months until established.

6. Once the behavior is established, and the cat spontaneously hops off the counter for clicks when she sees you coming, you can add in the spoken cue: "Off!" or "Floor, please!" when you want your cat to jump off.

7. Occasionally positively reinforce your cat simply being where you want her to be, namely on the floor or on the approved-by-you perch.

Key Elements/Things to keep in mind: Consider why your cat wants to be on the counter in the first place, and work with that. Mainly, two things: counters harbor food (or crumbs), and cats love high-up places because they feel safe and can survey their surroundings. Regarding food: never provide positive reinforcement by feeding on the "forbidden" counter or providing scraps to your cat while he's on the counter, and never leave food unattended. Also, clean up any crumbs or spills that might smell good to your cat. As for the high perch, provide a different high-up alternative that works for you, and that your cat likes.

BITING/CHEWING

Easy to intermediate

Biting and chewing are most often the result of play getting too boisterous. You can train your cat to play nice.

Materials:

- Treats
- Clicker

Hand Signal:

None.

Step-by-step:

1. Have your clicker and treats on you so that you can train on the fly, however, see "Key elements" below as reminder of how important the "do-nothing" strategy sometimes is in training too.

2. When you're playing with your cat and she starts to bite, chew or scratch, get up and walk away — this simply shows your cat that rough play ends the fun.

3. Be consistent. Don't walk away sometimes and allow your cat to roughhouse you other times. This comes down to intermittent reinforcement, which will make the problem worse.

4. After a few times of you exiting the game at the first sign of rough play, your cat may retract her claws and turn the play gentle when she notices you getting up to leave. If so, click and treat for gentle play, and stay in the game.

Key Elements/Things to keep in mind: When training cats to let go of problem behaviors, the clicker and treats are an important tool, but equally important is the very counterintuitive method of doing nothing in the face of bad behavior. For example, if your cat likes to stalk you and pounce — tooth and nail — on your ankles, stop. Stand still. You might want to duck and dive, but that's just making it more fun for your cat. Fun is positive reinforcement. You doing nothing is boring, and your cat is more likely to learn to give up and seek fun elsewhere.

CONSTANT MEOWING/ MEOWING FOR ATTENTION

Intermediate

Meowing might signal hunger, thirst or a need to use the toilet, but is often a request for attention. Responding to meowing by turning to your cat, speaking to him, opening a door or anything else amounts to attention, so it's likely to make meowing increase.

Materials:

- Treats
- Clicker

Hand Signal:

None.

Step-by-step:

1. Don't respond to attention-seeking meowing.

2. Give your cat attention when they're quiet — look for opportunities to do this throughout the day. Click and treat if you like.

3. Be mindful of your response to meowing. If you open the door for your cat when he meows, with the thought, "He must want something ... Is he asking me to open the door?" that's a surefire way to get your cat to meow whenever he wants the door opened. In other words, recognizing when you're reinforcing unwanted behaviors.

4. Do reinforce the vocalizations you like, such as chirruping to welcome you home, or chattering as you prepare their food.

Key Elements/Things to keep in mind: As with most of the training commands and behaviors, this training could be anything from very easy to pretty hard. The golden ingredient is patience. If you're patient and willing to follow the training steps whenever the behavior comes up, you will be rewarded. See how there's a great cycle of positive reinforcement: The cat does what you want, so you reward him. Then he rewards you by behaving the way you want more often. Then you reward him for being a good boy. Then he rewards you by being even better. And so on.

JUMPING UP

Easy to intermediate

Like counter surfing, this is a frequent undesired behavior that can unwittingly be reinforced by you. As long as you're patient and consistent, it's not difficult to train your cat out of jumping up onto tables and other out-of-bounds furniture. Target Touch needs to be fully established before you tackle this one.

Materials:

- Treats
- Clicker
- Target stick

Hand Signal:

None.

---

* Can only be done once Target Touch is successfully established.

Step-by-step:

1. Have your clicker and treats at the ready so you can train on the fly.

2. When your cat jumps up where he shouldn't be, lure him off with your target stick.

3. Click and reward as he lands on the ground.

4. As with counter surfing, if your cat jumps back up, do not scold or physically move him. Just use the target stick, and click and treat when he lands on the ground.

5. Repeat over days, weeks and months until established.

6. Once the behavior is established, you can add in the spoken cue: "Off!" or "Floor, please!"

Key Elements/Things to keep in mind: Consider why your cat wants to be on the counter in the first place, and work with that. Mainly, two things: counters harbor food (or crumbs), and cats love high-up places because they feel safe and can survey their surroundings. Regarding food: never provide positive reinforcement by feeding on the "forbidden" counter or providing scraps to your cat while he's on the counter, and never leave food unattended. Also, clean up any crumbs or spills that might smell good to your cat. As for the high perch, provide a different high-up alternative that works for you, and that your cat likes.

CHAPTER 6

CLICKER TRAINING FOR FUN AND ENRICHMENT

In this chapter, we shift our focus to the joys of clicker training for fun and enrichment. Having built a foundation with commands and behavior correction, you're ready to explore playful activities that harness your cat's natural curiosity and agility. These exercises are designed to be engaging for your cat and enjoyable for you, adding variety and mental stimulation to daily routines. Training for enrichment isn't just about tricks—it's about fostering a lively, interactive environment where your cat can express their instincts in rewarding ways.

From chasing dots to mastering the "Figure 8" leg weave, these games bring out the playful, sometimes acrobatic side of your feline friend. Each activity is a chance to strengthen your bond, deepen communication, and help your cat thrive both mentally and physically. Whether your goal is to encourage a spirited tunnel run or practice a game of "Guess the Hand," this chapter offers a toolkit of creative, accessible ways to make training a highlight of your cat's day.

GAMES

DOT CHASING (LASER POINTER)

Easy

So easy and so delightful, the treats and clicker are unlikely to be necessary. Note that a very small percentage of cats can't see the dot at all! This is possibly some quirk of vision. Most cats, however, will be all over the dot. In my house, we have three cats. Two of them gleefully play with the dot, while the third, a healthy, normal ginger boy, watches them, dumbfounded, with an expression of "What are you guys on about?" Clearly, Jasper can't see the dot.

Materials:

- Laser pointer
- Treats (optional)
- Clicker (optional)

Hand Signal:

None.

Step-by-step:

1. Begin by picking up laser pointer and bringing the dot out of its "hiding place." (See Key elements below.)

2. Now, simply point the dot at a surface you're happy for your cat to run on or swat at, and your cat will follow. The game is its own reward, so it's not likely you'll need to click or treat.

3. If your cat doesn't seem that interested, click and treat any movement towards the dot. It's likely they'll soon come around.

4. If your cat is one of the small handful of cats like Jasper, that literally can't see the dot, they will look confused or dumbfounded. In that case, just move on to the next trick.

Key Elements/Things to keep in mind: Some cats (and dogs) become so obsessed with the laser dot they keep looking for it all over the house. To prevent this, give the appearance of the dot context: at the beginning of the game pretend the dot is coming out from a specific place: Out of a special box, or out from under your shoe. At the end of the game, guide the dot back into this position as if you're putting it away.

GUESS THE HAND

Easy

This simple, easy game is not a showstopper: instead, its value lies in then strengthening of your bond with your cat. It's also a good way of introducing your cat to structured play, creating a foundation for the more complicated games. You can do this own on your own, or get a friend to help you with the treats.

Materials:

- Treats with a good amount of smell to them
- Clicker
- A friend or family member to help
- A toy that fits into your closed hand

Hand Signal:

None.

Step-by-step:

1. Begin seated on the ground beside your cat. The treats are in a container behind you — unless your cat is so intrigued by them that they keep trying to run behind you to grab some. In this case, get your friendly assistant to hold the treats out of the way. (This person is also holding the clicker.)

2. Put a treat in one hand and close both fists. Now hold out both hands, a little closer than shoulder width apart.

3. Your cat will come up to sniff your hands. When it sniffs at the correct hand (your assistant will) click. Then open your hand and let the cat have the treat. Ensure the click happens at the exact time of the sniff.

4. Repeat a few times, with different hands, to reinforce.

5 In a new session, or the same one, if your cat is still interested, start shaping a paw tap to your hand. The goal is for your cat, instead of just sniffing, to tap your hand to indicate "this one!" Therefore, no longer click and reward the sniffing, but wait for any movement of the paw towards the correct hand. Keep shaping this over many sessions if necessary until you have a nice paw tap.

6 Reinforce only gentle taps, not taps with claws out, or scratching. Don't reinforce any chewing of your hand.

7 Mix it up for a more advanced version. Sometimes, instead of the treat, put a small toy in your hand for the guessing game. Reward correct guesses with a click and treat, or some play time with the toy.

Key Elements/Things to keep in mind: This is a good way to get your cat interacting with kids, if you like, because it's a nice low-energy interaction and fun for both cat and kid.

PREY CHASING (CATCHING A FAKE MOUSE)

Easy

Cats have a natural instinct to hunt. This game is a great way for them to engage their prey drive without harming any wildlife.

Materials:
- Toy such as a fake mouse or feather wand

Hand Signal:
None.

Step-by-step:

1. Get your cat's attention by waving or waggling the toy a few inches in front of them.

2. Once your cat is interested, drag the toy across the floor, and watch them follow. They will soon chase and pounce. Let them.

3. Do not let your cat sink its claws or teeth into your hand: be mindful of how and where you're holding the toy, so you avoid fangs and nails.

4. If, despite your careful handling of the toy, your cat attacks your hand, simply stop the game. Don't scold or cause drama: simply remove the toy and go do something else. This avoids reinforcing biting and scratching.

Key Elements/Things to keep in mind: Like chasing the laser pointer, this game is so fun and easy it can be used almost any time as a reward in itself, or to mix things up when your cat has lost interest in some other aspect of training or is finding a new concept challenging.

BELL RINGING

Easy to intermediate

Loads of fun, and a great way to impress friends.

Materials:

- Treats
- Clicker
- Target stick
- A service bell (as seen on front desk counters, etc)

Hand Signal:

None.

Step-by-step:

1. Sit on the floor beside your cat, with the bell next to her. Using the lure, guide her paw to the bell. This action is likely to need shaping. Your goal is getting your cat to whack her paw onto the top of the bell, so reinforce movement of the paw towards the bell, and then onto the top of the bell, and then for increasing pressure onto the button, and so on.

2. Click and treat the successes as you shape.

3. Once your cat is spontaneously whacking the bell when she sees it, at you cue words: "Bell!" or "Ring the bell!" now only clicking for ringing that happens on cue.

Key Elements/Things to keep in mind: You could use a cue action instead of a cue word, like this. Imagine you only want your cat do ring the bell as if she's asking for her dinner. Then you could make you placing you cat's empty bowl beside the bell the cue. Click and treat as always, to reinforce, and, finally, serve that kitty dinner she's been ringing for!

FETCH

Intermediate

This game is mentally stimulating and a fun way for your cat to get exercise indoors.

Materials:

- Treats
- Clicker
- Cat toy, such as a felt mouse
- Target stick

Hand Signal:

None.

Step-by-step:

1. Ensure the toy is one your cat can easily carry in his mouth, and make it a special one that you don't leave lying around the house. This makes it more interesting to your cat.

2. Hold the toy a few inches from your cat's face, and click and reward when he shows interest, for example, sniffing the toy.

3. The next part to shape is getting him to open his mouth, and hold the toy in his mouth. Click and reward all progress towards this step.

4. Next, shape dropping the toy. This could take a while for your cat to get, and you might very well happen for the moment where the toy gets dropped by coincidence.

5. The next aspect to bake into this recipe is distance: Take the toy and toss it a few inches away. Your cat is likely to follow.

6. Now, using your target stick, lure your cat back to you. At this point you want your cat to drop the toy again: you could simply hold out a treat in your hand, which will elicit the desired action. Immediately click, and give the treat.

Key Elements/Things to keep in mind:

A. In some aspects of training, for example getting the cat to drop the toy in "Fetch," what you're asking the cat might not make much sense to him. In cases like these, you need to capitalize on those random moments when they "get it right" — which is usually a matter of coincidence. In this case, the cat just happens to finally drop the toy. Rejoice! Now click and treat immediately.

B. With this one, the order of the middle steps is up to you: play it by ear to see which order will work for you and your cat.

TUNNEL RUN

Easy

This is a fun game out of the book of dog agility training, and another great one for indoor exercise.

Materials:

- Treats
- Clicker
- Target stick
- Pet toy tunnel (usually made of cloth)
- Cat toy or ball of scrunched paper

Hand Signal:

None.

Step-by-step:

1. Put out the tunnel and let your cat investigate it for some minutes, until she seems comfortable with it.

2. Show your cat the toy or paper ball. Now throw it through the tunnel and watch her follow!

3. Click at the moment she enters the tunnel. You could offer a treat when she comes out the other side, but it's likely she'll be having some pretty energetic play with the toy, which is its own reward.

4. Repeat several times. If you want to see her do this move on cue, wait until the move is established and she does it for her own amusement, then add the cue: "Tunnel run!"

Key Elements/Things to keep in mind: The tunnel run relies on natural playfulness to such an extent that you might want to forego the cue and just let your cat do what comes naturally. In this case, the simple fact of the tunnel being set up is the cue/invitation to play.

HURDLE JUMP

Easy to intermediate

A very natural cat behavior that's really fun to see on cue. Great for strength and conditioning, and another good one for indoor exercise.

Materials:

- Treats
- Clicker
- An obstacle one or two feet high, such as an upturned box or plastic container on its side
- Target stick

Hand Signal:

None.

Step-by-step:

1. Position the obstacle in a suitable position on the floor. Put the target stick in your hand: it's there to entice the cat over the obstacle, when she could just as easily go around.

2. Lead your cat up and over, using the target stick.

3. Click at the moment your cat jumps up.

4. Repeat to reinforce.

5. Once your cat hurdles all by herself, you can add the cue: "Hurdle jump!" This can help contain hurdling to the times and places you ask for it.

Key Elements/Things to keep in mind: The hurdle exercise is a warm-up to the chair leap. Since the hurdle jump is lower, it's a good place to start.

CHAIR LEAPS

Intermediate

Everyone knows cats are natural acrobats, but seeing the acrobatics happen on cue will impress your friends.

Materials:

- Treats
- Clicker
- A series of stackable objects, such as boxes, to increase height bit by bit
- Chair
- Target stick

Hand Signal:

None.

Step-by-step:

1. Begin by placing two or so boxes on top of each other. You want a height greater than for the hurdle jump, but a lot lower, for now, than the chair. Ensure the arrangement is sturdy: You don't want anything crashing down at any point in the jump.

2. Using your target stick, lead the cat to jump over the stack.

3. Click at the moment your cat jumps up.

4. Repeat to reinforce.

5. Gradually, over different sessions, increase the height of the stack until it's almost as high as the chair back.

6. Once your cat is happy with that height, you can replace your training stack with the actual chair.

7. Once your cat does the chair leap all by herself, you can add the cue: "Chair leap!"

Key Elements/Things to keep in mind: Technically, this is extremely easy for your cat. In his own time, he'll clear far greater heights all by himself. But it's a different matter when you're asking him to do it for you, in a training set-up.

FIGURE 8 LEG WEAVE

Intermediate

This is something your cat quite likely already does, only at completely inopportune moments, like when you're cooking dinner or carrying heavy bags of groceries. Here's your chance to teach her to do it on cue.

Materials:

- Treats
- Clicker
- Target stick

Hand Signal:

None.

Step-by-step:

1. Stand on the floor with your cat at your feet. Use the target stick to lead your cat around your legs. If initially she doesn't seem interested, remember to reward even small movements in the direction you're after.

2. Keep building the move in increments, until you have the complete Figure 8.

3. Once you have the full move, add your cue: "Weave!" At this point, you no longer need the target stick.

Key Elements/Things to keep in mind: By this stage, your cat is used to having the target stick lead her all over. See what a useful tool this has become, and it all started with Target Touch — which might have seemed so boring or random at the time!

CHAPTER 7
WRAPPING UP

By this point in your clicker training journey, you and your cat might be doing some things together that on Day 1 would have seemed way advanced. Now is a good time to pull it all together by pausing at the basics again for a moment.

Benefits of clicker training: a recap

The importance of lifelong mental and physical stimulation for cats

Most domestic cats are pretty far removed from nature and from the lifestyle their instincts dictate. What's more, in terms of physical needs, pet cats are totally catered for. Not only do (a lot of) cats not have access to hunting, they have no need for it in terms of calories.

Being taken care of in terms of food, water and shelter leaves house cats with a lot of extra time and energy, which could lead to that energy being directed into unwanted behaviors. This is true at all life stages, and not just in kittenhood.

Clicker training provides both mental and physical stimulation. The mental part is where the cat gets to figure out what the behavior is you're rewarding, and that he should repeat that behavior. Training that involves shaping is also great mental stimulation. Games, tricks and play add the physical element.

The benefits of positive reinforcement training for cats and their owners

When it comes to learning, positive reinforcement is one of the most successful strategies around — not only for animals, but also for people. The simple alternative is punishment.

Cast your mind back to some memorable learning moments of your own, for example Grade 3 math class. Remember learning your times tables? Which was more effective: you get an answer wrong, and the teacher whacks you with a ruler, or you get one wrong, and they ignore the error, but give you a high five for the right answer?

Fortunately most younger readers might not have direct experience of getting whacked by their math teacher, but you can picture the scene. It's blatantly obvious that the high five for the correct answer — positive reinforcement — has better outcomes.

In positive-reinforcement training the student (your cat) and the teacher (you) both get to feel rewarded. Both of you get the dopamine flowing with each little success, and there's no getting mad, no sulking, and no erosion of self-esteem. And, if you do ever find yourself getting mad or frustrated, that's a sign to pack it up for the day and try again tomorrow.

The versatility and adaptability of clicker training for different cats and situations

As you've seen throughout this book, you can use the clicker to teach your cat to do everything from allowing themselves to be groomed, to sitting still as you prepare their dinner, to jumping through a hoop.

Since the sound of the clicker marks the moment, and therefore marks the behavior or action you want your cat to repeat, you can use it to teach a really wide variety of things.

While food is the classic training reward, it is certainly possible to use affection (e.g. chin tickles, jaw scratches, or a light massage down the sides of your cat's spine) as reward. Play is also a great reward. These non-food rewards are good for any cat, but especially for cats that need their weight managed.

Encouragement to continue training and building a positive relationship with your cat

The long-term benefits for training for both you and your cat

If done consistently and with real attention to the positive reinforcement aspect, clicker training is sure to strengthen the bond between you and your cat. As long as you adhere to the principles, and never use punishment, you will be building the trust between you and your cat.

TIPS FOR KEEPING TRAINING SESSIONS ENJOYABLE AND REWARDING FOR BOTH YOU AND YOUR CAT

- Respect your cat's attention span: keep training sessions short.
- Don't put pressure on yourself or your cat. Results take time, and every cat is different.
- Have delicious treats on hand. You can't expect your cat to perform for bland scraps like dry kibble.
- Remember that cuddles are a reward too! Terms and conditions apply. (Meaning, read your cat's body language to figure out whether at this moment cuddles are desired or not.)
- Consider keeping a log of your training, noting what you did, and the progress you made, however miniscule.
- Always be patient.
- If you're an A-type personality, take a deep breath and remind yourself that yes, patience is a virtue.
- Train in a space free of distractions. Most people or other pets would be a distraction.

Ideas for continuing to build a strong bond with your cat through training and other activities

Challenge yourself by thinking of your cat's own specific situation: what training would enrich her? What training would help with her safety? What games would amuse her most?

If you live in a high-rise apartment building, teaching your cat to walk on a leash would enrich her. If you have a new puppy who likes to chase running cats, you might want to teach her to not run, but sit down on seeing the puppy, thereby making her as boring as a piece of lettuce.

Do use your discretion in terms of safety for all (each cat is different, and each puppy is different, and some puppies grow into bull mastiffs ...) Also, in the case of introducing a new pet to the household, absolutely train the new pet too!

While punishment doesn't gel with positive reinforcement, the idea is not to just be "nice" all the time: when your cat doesn't do what you're trying to teach, you can always remove something it wants, as a sort of anti-reward.

For example, if you're trying to teach your cat not to knead you with sharp, prickly nails when she comes in for lap time, when she sinks her claws into your flesh you're going to gently pick her up, put her aside and then you walk away. That's removing the thing she wanted at that moment: time on your lap.

TIPS AND BEST PRACTICES FOR MAINTAINING AND ENHANCING THE POSITIVE RELATIONSHIP BETWEEN YOU AND YOUR CAT THROUGH TRAINING AND OTHER ACTIVITIES:

USEFUL TIPS

- Reward wanted behavior.
- For "fails" or "misses" simply don't respond.
- Never punish.
- Reward even tiny movements in the right direction.
- For undesired behaviors, try to see from your cat's perspective. If you can figure out why your cat is doing something in the first place, you can rectify the situation in a way that works with your cat's needs, not against. (See Chapter 5: Problem Behaviors.)

Resources for further learning and support

Recommended books, websites and online communities

Decoding Your Cat: The Ultimate Experts Explain Common Cat Behaviors and Reveal How to Prevent or Change Unwanted Ones by the American College of Veterinary Behaviorists, Boston: Houghton Mifflin Harcourt, 2020

Professional organizations or certifications related to feline training and behavior

American Association of Feline Practitioners
https://catvets.com/cfp/cat-friendly-certificate-program/

IAABC
https://iaabc.org

IAABC Foundation
https://iaabcfoundation.org

Karen Pryor Academy
https://karenpryoracademy.com

Toronto Humane Society
https://www.torontohumanesociety.com/pet-services/training-and-behaviour/cat-training-and-consultations/

Options for seeking additional help or support, such as consulting with a veterinarian or a certified animal behaviorist

Despite your best efforts in training, some challenges may remain. In such cases, you might want to reach out for additional help or support, such as consulting with a veterinarian or certified animal behaviorist. The decision tree below may assist.

How to choose the appropriate resource or support

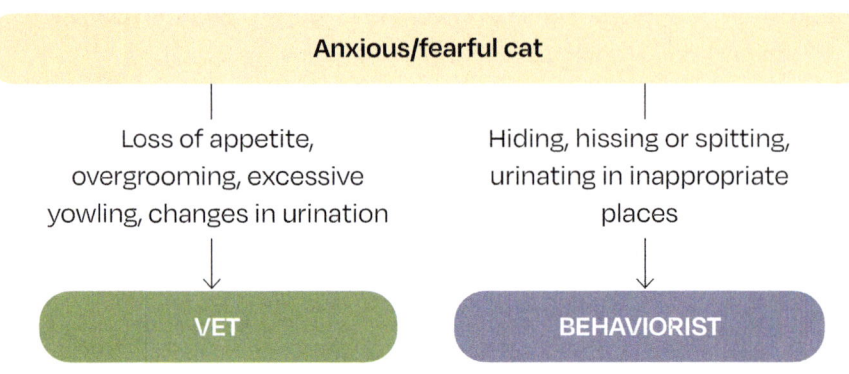

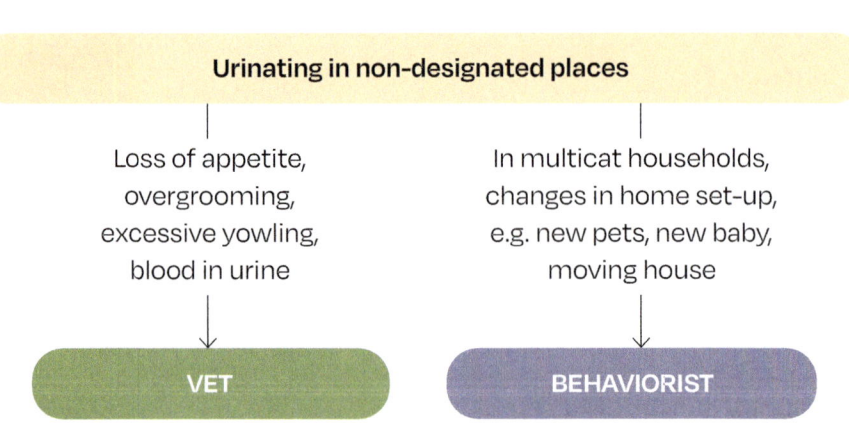

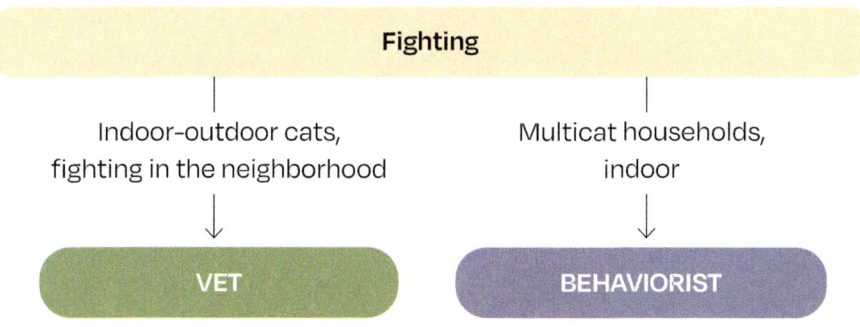

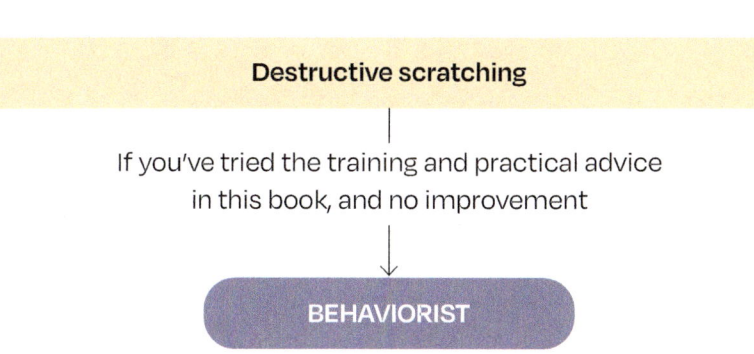

Printed in Dunstable, United Kingdom

64948154R10080